TAILS DON'T LIE

TAILS DON'T LIE 2

A Pack of Dog Cartoons

ADRIAN RAESIDE

HARBOUR PUBLISHING

This book is dedicated to anyone who has rescued an animal.

Koko, a rescue dog, and his best buddy, Sakura, brought endless joy and inspiration. They have both since passed over to the Rainbow Bridge but they live on in our hearts and in The Other Coast.

1 2 3 4 5 — 21 20 19 18 17

HARBOUR PUBLISHING CO. LTD.
P.O. Box 219, Madeira Park, BC,
V0N 2H0, Canada
www.harbourpublishing.com

Book cover and page layout
by Teresa Karbashewski.

This book was printed with soy-based inks on chlorine-free paper made from 10% post-consumer waste.

Printed and bound in Canada.

Library and Archives Canada Cataloguing in Publication

Raeside, Adrian, 1957-
[Cartoons. Selections]
Tails don't lie 2 : a pack of dog cartoons / Adrian Raeside.
Issued in print and electronic formats.

ISBN 978-1-55017-793-0 (softcover).–ISBN 978-1-55017-794-7 (HTML)

1. Dogs–Caricatures and cartoons. 2. Canadian wit and humor, Pictorial. I. Title. II. Title: Tails do not lie two.

NC1449.R34A4 2017 741.5'6971 C2016-907502-8
C2016-907503-6

Harbour Publishing acknowledges the support of the Canada Council for the Arts, which last year invested $153 million to bring the arts to Canadians throughout the country. We also gratefully acknowledge financial support from the Government of Canada through the Canada Book Fund and from the Province of British Columbia through the BC Arts Council and the Book Publishing Tax Credit.

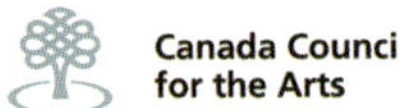

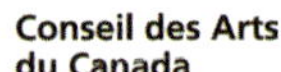

Introduction

I've always thought dogs' tails are fascinating. They're so incredibly versatile. They use them to communicate everything from the furious, full-body-wiggling "I'm so happy to see you I could burst!" wag, the side-to-side "I'm not sure who you are but I'm pretty sure I smell a treat in your pocket" wag, and the "N-O-O-O! Is that the vet's office we're pulling up to?" under-the-bum tuck. They also keep noses warm on cold nights (unless they have been docked) and they are excellent at conveniently sweeping food off low tables.

Tails Don't Lie 2 features the philosophical, ditch-wading, farting, shedding, bed-hogging, hairy scroungers who inhabit my *Other Coast* comic strip. They reveal why dogs covet the driver's seat, what would happen if dogs went on space missions (do aliens have dogs?), the humiliation of tail-docking, if purebreds are really canine snobs, the immense importance of trees to a dog, and ask the eternal question: Why isn't squirrel-chasing included in dog agility courses?

If you have a dog, I hope you will spot yours in *Tails Don't Lie 2*. If you don't have a dog, visit your local animal shelter. There's a dog there waiting for you. And, as anyone who has rescued a dog will tell you, rescue dogs give the best face-licks!

—ADRIAN RAESIDE

DOG GPS
CONTINUE ON THIS HEADING FOR THE NEXT... SQUIRREL!
RAESIDE

MY GREAT-GREAT-GREAT-GRANDDOG BARRY RAN OFF TO SEA ON A PIRATE SHIP.
PIRATES

IT DIDN'T TURN OUT TOO WELL, AS BARRY HAD AN ANNOYING HABIT OF CHEWING STUFF.
LIKE WHAT?
RATES

"LIKE THE SHIP."
RAESIDE

WELL, HELLOOO THERE. ALLOW ME TO INTRODUCE MYSELF. I AM A WOLF.

OH, MY.
YEP, I'M PRETTY MUCH NUMERO UNO AROUND HERE.

DON'T WASTE YOUR TIME WITH HIM, DORIS. HE'S ACTUALLY JUST A COYOTE.
I PREFER TO THINK OF MYSELF AS "WOLF LITE."
RAESIDE

NOTHING LIKE A HIKE UP MOUNT McNASTY.

HERE WE ARE, KOKO. THE BARREN, ROCKY PEAK OF McNASTY.

DRINK IN THE VIEWS, AND INHALE THE FRESH AIR. WHAT MORE COULD ONE WANT?

RAESIDE
A STICK WOULD BE NICE.

I'M IN THE BACK SEAT, GOING FOR A CAR RIDE.

I AM THE COOLEST DOG IN THE WORLD!

RAESIDE

BIG RUSTY, THE EX-POLICE DOG. HOW'S RETIREMENT?
LOUSY. I MESSED UP, AND NOW I'M BEING SENT BACK FOR DEPROGRAMMING.

RAESIDE
WHAT DID YOU DO?
MY DAD TOOK ME SKIING, AND I TOOK DOWN A BUNCH OF SKIERS. HARD.

IT WAS AN INSTINCTIVE REACTION. THEY WERE WEARING SKI MASKS.

HAVE YOU NOTICED JOGGERS NEVER LOOK HAPPY?
UNLIKE THEIR DOGS.

I'M GOING TO SNEAK OUT TO THE MALL WITHOUT KOKO NOTICING...

AND SO HE DOESN'T HEAR KEYS JINGLING, I'M ONLY CARRYING THE CAR KEY.

I CAN SMELL CAR KEYS.

HERE'S A PHOTO OF MY MOM. GOLLY. I STILL MISS HER AFTER ALL THESE YEARS.

IT'S NOT FAIR. PEOPLE HAVE PHOTOS TO REMEMBER THEIR MOMS BY; DOGS ONLY HAVE SMELLS.

"THAT'S HOW I REMEMBER MY MOM: HER DELICATE SCENT OF WARM HAIR, NUTMEG, LILAC AND MUDDY DITCH."

MUDDY DITCH?
MOM DIDN'T LIKE BATHS, EITHER.

I THINK THEY'RE HOME. I'LL JUST RING THE DOORBELL...

RAESIDE

BARK! BARK! BARK! BARK!

TV NETWORKS RUN "COARSE LANGUAGE" AND "VIOLENCE" WARNINGS. WHY CAN'T THEY ADD A "DOORBELL" WARNING?

RAESIDE

THAT'S POINTLESS, SITTING IN THE DRIVER'S SEAT OF A CAR THAT'S IN PIECES.
AS LONG AS THE DRIVER'S SEAT IS INTACT, THAT'S ALL THAT MATTERS.

WELL, HELLO, TROY. YOU'RE LOOKING GOOD!
OH, HI, JEWELL.

SO, WHAT SAY YOU AND ME GO BACK TO MY KENNEL?
NAH. I'M HEADING HOME TO THE COUCH.

SO, ER, GIVE ME A BARK SOMETIME?
YEAH, MAYBE.

DAYTIME SOAPS JUST AREN'T THE SAME AFTER THE LEADING DOG GETS NEUTERED.

I ONLY BUY EXPENSIVE PREMIUM DOG FOOD FOR MAX. I'M VERY PARTICULAR ABOUT HIS DIET.
RAESIDE

BARK BARK BARK BARK BARK BARK!

ARE YOU NUTS? HE'S TEN TIMES YOUR SIZE.
RELAX. HE'S A GUIDE DOG. HE'S NOT ALLOWED TO RESPOND TO TAUNTS.

RAESIDE
JUST WAIT UNTIL I RETIRE...

I CAN PROVE RUSTY ROBBED THE BANK. THE NOSE PRINTS WE LIFTED OFF THE TELLER'S WINDOW MATCH RUSTY'S NOSE EXACTLY!
RAESIDE

WELL? AREN'T YOU GOING TO TAKE HIM DOWN?
ONE OF MY NEW YEAR'S RESOLUTIONS WAS TO BE NICER TO PEOPLE.
RAESIDE

"DISTRESSING" FURNITURE IS A WAY TO MAKE ORDINARY FURNITURE LOOK ANTIQUE.

TO GET THAT SCRATCHED, BATTERED LOOK, ALL YOU NEED IS SANDPAPER, CHISEL AND WIRE BRUSH.

OR YOU COULD JUST GET A PUPPY.
I ASSUMED A COFFEE TABLE WOULD BE COFFEE-FLAVORED.
RAESIDE

I'M AT THE STAGE IN MY LIFE WHEN I START TO REGRET THE GOALS I NEVER ACHIEVED.

YOU MEAN LIKE BEING THE FIRST DOG ON THE MOON OR CLIMBING MOUNT EVEREST?

I WAS THINKING MORE LIKE SNEAKING ONTO THE BED MORE OFTEN.
IF YOU SET THE BAR ANY LOWER, YOU'D HAVE TO DIG FOR IT.
RAESIDE

LOOK, SAKURA. I BOUGHT YOU A RUBBER SQUEAKY RAT.
WHAAT?!

THIS IS INSULTING. JUST BECAUSE MY ANCESTORS WERE RATTERS, YOU ASSUME I AM, TOO.

MY BREED HAS EVOLVED. YOUR TAWDRY REPRESENTATION OF THE PAST HOLDS NO INTEREST FOR THIS DOG.

RAESIDE
BUT I THOUGHT...
I'M ADDICTED TO SQUEAKS.

CUTE PUPPY. HOW'S THE TRAINING GOING?
PRETTY GOOD. I'VE GOT HIM SNEAKING ME SCRAPS OFF THE TABLE, AND I'M NOW ALLOWED TO SLEEP ON THE COUCH. WE'RE STILL WORKING ON ME SLEEPING ON THE BED.
RAESIDE

"... AND NEXT UP IN THE TERRIER CATEGORY, JIMMY LUCKY SOCKS."

JIMMY IS A TWO-TIME STATE-LEVEL WINNER.
HELLO?

RAESIDE
THERE'S A FLEA ON HIS EAR!

THAT'S THE PROBLEM WITH HDTV. YOU CAN SEE EVERYTHING.

RAESIDE
IS THAT A PUPPY?
YEP, HE'S AN AVALANCHE RESCUE DOG IN TRAINING.

HE'S TEAMED UP WITH AN OLDER, EXPERIENCED RESCUE DOG TO LEARN THE ROPES.

FIRST THING YOU DO IS GO THROUGH THEIR POCKETS, LOOKING FOR SNACKS.

RAESIDE
GET IN THERE AND ORDER TWO TABBIES TO GO.
CAT CAFÉ
TEA, COFFEE AND CATS

I BOUGHT ONE OF THOSE SILENT DOG WHISTLES.
I HAVE ONE, TOO.

I'LL CALL MY DOG.
I'LL CALL MINE, TOO.

RAESIDE
IS THAT ME?
WAS THAT WHISTLE FOR ME?
IT MIGHT HAVE BEEN MY WHISTLE.
THEY ALL SOUND THE SAME TO ME.

RAESIDE
OH, COME ON. THERE'S NO NEED TO SHOUT.
NO
DOGS ALLOWED IN STORE

RAESIDE

TRYING TO LOSE WEIGHT, VICTOR?
MY GOAL IS TO BE ABLE TO FIT THROUGH THE DOG DOOR.

RAESIDE
OPEN
DOG REAL ESTATE
LUXURY COUCH
PRICE REDUCED
FIXER-UPPER
STARTER COUCH

HAVE YOU EVER WONDERED IF ALIENS HAVE LANDED AND ARE LIVING AMONG US?

I'M SURE THEY HAVE. IN FACT, I ONCE DETECTED ONE.

"I NOTICED A GUY WHO HAD A PECULIAR ODOR..."
HMM... I SMELL CROP CIRCLES...
RAESIDE

GOLLY. DID YOU TURN HIM IN?
NO WAY! HE HAD A POCKET-FUL OF ALIEN DOG BISCUITS.

"DOGGO" DOG BISCUITS, BECAUSE YOUR PET DESERVES THE VERY BEST!

FOR THOSE OBNOXIOUS DOG ODORS, USE "WHIZZO" AIR FRESHENERS.

AND NOW, BACK TO OUR MOVIE.

RAESIDE
PEOPLE ON TV ARE WEIRD. THEY EITHER LOVE US OR THEY HATE US.

DAD HAS GONE SHOPPING, SO I WILL NOW STARE INTENTLY AT THE STORE HE WENT INTO.

HE THINKS I'M STARING AT THE STORE BECAUSE I MISS HIM. BUT THAT'S NOT THE CASE AT ALL...

I WANT TO SPOT HIM AS SOON AS HE LEAVES THE STORE SO I CAN JUMP OUT OF THE DRIVER'S SEAT WITHOUT HIM KNOWING I WAS HERE.

RAESIDE
AHEM!
OH, THAT IS SO SNEAKY!

HI, I'M KOKO. WHAT'S YOUR NAME?
EDDIE. I'M PLEASED TO MEET YOU.
RAESIDE

YOU DON'T SEEM PLEASED.
NO, REALLY, I AM PLEASED.

OH, SORRY, I DIDN'T NOTICE YOUR TAIL WAS DOCKED.
I WAS WAGGING MY STUMP.

...AND AS AN ADDED BONUS, WITH YOUR MAGAZINE SUBSCRIPTION, WE'RE INCLUDING A BONE-SHAPED BISCUIT THAT NOBODY EVER GETS BECAUSE RUSTY IN SHIPPING GETS TO IT FIRST.
RAESIDE

WHEN I WAS A POLICE DOG, I WAS AN EXPERT IN SEEING THROUGH DISGUISES.
RAESIDE

"I'VE SPOTTED BANK ROBBERS HIDING BEHIND FALSE BEARDS..."

"I'VE EVEN CAUGHT BANK ROBBERS DISGUISED AS CLOWNS!"

AND YOUR MOST MEMORABLE COLLAR?
A ROBBER DRESSED AS A SQUIRREL.

WHAT ARE YOU DOING AT THE TABLE? NOT BEGGING, I HOPE.
NOPE, PURE COINCIDENCE. I JUST HAPPENED TO BE IN THE NEIGHBOR-HOOD.

YES, YOU ARE. YOU'RE GIVING ME THAT "SAD EYES" LOOK!
ACTUALLY, IT'S MY "STARVING TO DEATH" LOOK, BUT AGAIN, PURE COINCIDENCE.

WHAT DO YOU THINK WOULD HAPPEN IF AN EARTH-KILLING ASTEROID WAS DISCOVERED?

"I BET WE'D BUILD A FLEET OF SPACESHIPS TO CARRY US TO ANOTHER PLANET."

GOLLY, I SURE HOPE THEY'LL TAKE THEIR PETS WITH THEM!

OF COURSE THEY WILL. ALTHOUGH, I'M NOT SURE OF THE LOGISTICS OF A CAT BOX IN ZERO GRAVITY.

WE HAVE "THE DOG DAYS OF SUMMER." DO WE ALSO HAVE "THE DOG DAYS OF WINTER?"

AND IF THERE IS SUCH A THING, HOW WOULD WE KNOW IT WAS HERE?

OH, THERE ARE SOME SUBTLE SIGNS...

RAESIDE

YOU SPENT THE ENTIRE MORNING CHASING MICE? YOU'RE PATHETIC.
I PREFER TO THINK OF THEM AS PRACTICE SQUIRRELS.

OOH, I SHOULD GET THAT BALL SITTING OUT ON THIS FROZEN POND.

"BUT THE ICE COULD BE TOO THIN, AND I MIGHT FALL IN."
RAESIDE

"AND IF MY DAD TRIES TO RESCUE ME, HE MIGHT ALSO FALL IN."

DIDN'T WANT THAT BALL AFTER ALL?
WE DON'T WANT TO BE THE LEAD ON THE EVENING NEWS.

OH, BOY. I'M IN THE FRONT SEAT. THE OTHER DOGS WILL BE SO JEALOUS WHEN THEY SEE ME.

RAESIDE

COULD YOU DRIVE AROUND THE BLOCK ONE MORE TIME? NO DOGS SAW ME.

C'MON, KOKO, LET'S GO!

YOU'VE NEVER HEARD OF THE 15-SECOND SNIFF RULE?

A COUPLE OF BIRDS FLYING AROUND, CHATTERING TO EACH OTHER...

SQUIRRELS RACING ACROSS THE LAWN, THE COLLIE FROM DOWN THE STREET...

A WINDOW IS A SHUT-IN DOG'S TV.

AFTER THE AVALANCHE, MONTY THE AVALANCHE-RESCUE DOG GOES INTO ACTION.

GOT SOMETHING HERE!

I THINK IT'S TIME YOU WENT IN FOR A REFRESHER COURSE.
OH, RIGHT. I'M SUPPOSED TO FIND THE PERSON ATTACHED TO THIS.

the OTHER COAST

AWW, PHOOEY! I CAN'T FIND THIS BALL, EITHER.

WASN'T IT FUN PLAYING IN THE SNOW?

NO IT WASN'T. IT WAS A FIASCO OF EPIC PROPORTIONS.

WHAT A TERRIBLE MORNING. NO MATTER HOW HARD I TRIED, I WASN'T ABLE TO FIND A SINGLE BALL DAD THREW.

I'VE LOST MY HUNTING INSTINCT. I'M WASHED UP. AN EMBARASSMENT TO MY BREED.

WHAT KIND OF BALLS WERE YOU LOOKING FOR?

WHITE, ICY-LOOKING BALLS.

NO WONDER YOU COULDN'T FIND THEM, THEY WERE SNOWBALLS.

YOU MEAN I JUST SPENT A WHOLE MORNING IN THE SNOW LOOKING FOR BALLS MADE OF SNOW?

SNOWBALL THROWS ARE AS UNFAIR AS FAKE THROWS.

the OTHER COAST
RAESIDE
TO REDUCE GREEN-HOUSE GAS EMISSIONS, THE WORLD LOOKS TO ALTERNATE ENERGY SOURCES...

LIKE WIND...

SUN...

RIVERS...

EVEN ALGAE! HOWEVER, ALL THESE OPTIONS CAN COME AT A BIG PRICE. BUT THERE IS ONE UNTAPPED ENERGY SOURCE THAT IS BOTH LIMITLESS AND FREE...

...DOG HAIR.
YOU'RE WELCOME.

YOU CAN LIE AROUND THE HOUSE ALL DAY. I'M GOING OUTSIDE. I'VE HEARD THE CALL OF THE WILD.
the OTHER COAST

RAESIDE
SURE, I LIKE CATERED MEALS AND COMFY BEDS, BUT DEEP DOWN, I'M STILL A WILD ANIMAL.

BROUM!

HOW WAS THE CALL OF THE WILD?
IT WAS A WRONG NUMBER.

BARK BARK BARK
BARK BARK BARK
BARK

YOU COULDN'T HAVE JUST WAGGED YOUR TAIL AT HIM?
I DID, BUT HE BARKED AT ME, SO I BARKED BACK, AND, WELL, YOU KNOW HOW IT GOES...

A SUDDEN STENCH FILLED THE CROWDED ELEVATOR. BUT WHO WAS RESPONSIBLE...?

07

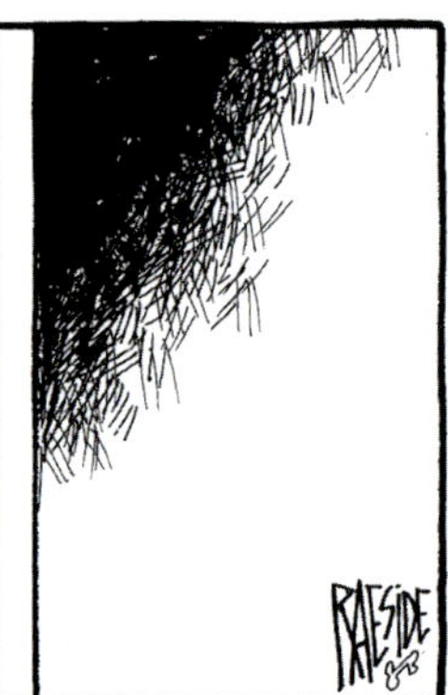

LOOK, SOME KIDS HAVE BUILT A SNOWMAN.

RAISINS FOR EYES, A CARROT FOR A NOSE AND STICKS FOR ARMS.

A BLATANT MISUSE OF STICKS.

RAESIDE
KOKO, WERE YOU SLEEPING ON THE BED THIS AFTERNOON?
UMM... NO.

SURE LOOKED LIKE DOG HAIR ON THE BED.
MUST HAVE BLOWN IN FROM OUTSIDE.

AND THE COMFORTER WAS ALL MUSSED UP.
SLOPPY BED-MAKING IF YOU ASK ME.

AND HOW DO YOU EXPLAIN DOG DROOL ON THE PILLOW?
RATTED OUT BY A CHEESE-COVERED SQUIRREL DREAM.

RAESIDE
DISCOUNT MAGIC ACTS:
I WILL NOW PLACE THIS DOG FOOD IN THIS BOWL, AND PRESTO!. RIGHT BEFORE YOUR VERY EYES, IT WILL DISAPPEAR!

WHATCHA WRITING, KOKO?

RAESIDE
A DETECTIVE NOVEL. THE HERO DETECTIVE HAS TO SOLVE A JEWEL HEIST.

AH, THE MOST NOBLE OF ALL GENRES. HOW DOES HE FIND THE THIEF? FORENSIC EVIDENCE OR JUST CUNNING DEDUCTIONS?

HE FOLLOWS THE TRAIL OF MUDDY PAW PRINTS.
SIR ARTHUR CONAN DOYLE IS ROLLING OVER IN HIS GRAVE.

CLIMATE SCIENTISTS WARN OF THE ECONOMIC IMPACT OF CLIMATE CHANGE.
CLIMATE
CHANGE

AS THE EARTH'S ATMOSPHERE WARMS, MOUNTAINS COULD SEE LESS SNOW...

THROWING SKI HILL EMPLOYEES OUT OF WORK.
ALONG WITH AVALANCHE RESCUE DOGS.
RAESIDE

THAT'S WILLIE.
HAVEN'T I SEEN HIM SOMEWHERE BEFORE?

"HE WAS THE DOG ON THE 5-POUND BAG OF DOGGO DOG FOOD."
RAESIDE
DOGGO
DOG FOOD
5 lbs

SINCE THEN, HE HAS PUT ON A BIT OF WEIGHT.
SO, HE WAS DROPPED FROM THE DOG FOOD BAGS?

"NOPE. HE WAS PUT ON THE 25-POUND BAG."
DOGGO
DOG FOOD
25 lbs

RAESIDE
A HINT OF PINE FOREST, NOTES OF WOOD SMOKE, WITH A STRONG MOWN GRASS FINISH.

A CAR RIDE IS LIKE TASTING A FINE WINE.

HEY, HERE'S A PHOTO OF ME WHEN I WAS IN THE OBEDIENCE SCHOOL PLAY.

RAESIDE
COOL. WHAT PART DID YOU PLAY?
A TREE.

IT WAS THE MOST HORRIBLE EXPERIENCE OF MY LIFE!

WHAT'S SO HORRIBLE ABOUT BEING A TREE?
EVERYONE ELSE ON THE STAGE WAS A DOG.

RAESIDE
LASSIE, GO GET HELP. GOOD GIRL!
BARK!
OH, PUH-LEASE!

EVERY "LASSIE" EPISODE IS THE SAME. TIMMY GETS TRAPPED IN A CAVE. LASSIE GETS HELP. TIMMY IS SAVED. THE END.

NOT THIS EPISODE. IT'S THE DIRECTOR'S CUT.
WHAT'S THE DIRECTOR'S CUT?

LASSIE HITCHES A RIDE TO LA, WHERE SHE BECOMES AN OUTDOOR CATALOG DOG, AND TIMMY GETS EATEN BY RATS.
LASSIE? THERE IS SOMETHING IN THE CAVE...

AUTHORITIES HAVE RAIDED A PUPPY MILL, SEIZING DOZENS OF DOGS.

DISEASED AND NEGLECTED, THEY WERE CRAMMED INTO TINY CRATES, LIVING IN DEPLORABLE CONDITIONS.

RAESIDE
THEY SHOULD PUT THE PEOPLE WHO RAN THAT PUPPY MILL IN JAIL.
THEY SHOULD PUT THEM IN THOSE CRATES.

DOG MOVIE REVIEWS:
I LOVED THIS MOVIE. I LAUGHED, I HOWLED! AT WHICH POINT, I WAS ASKED TO LEAVE THE THEATER.
RAESIDE

I KNOW, BUT THIS VERSION HAS SO MUCH MORE CLASS.
ROULETTE-PLAYING DOGS
RAESIDE

KOKO, YOU DON'T WANT TO GO FOR A WALK. IT'S POURING RAIN OUTSIDE.
DON'T CARE. I WANT TO GO OUTSIDE.

NO, REALLY, IT'S BLOWING A GALE, HAIL, FLOODS... IT'S A MESS OUT THERE!
YEAH, YEAH, LET'S GET GOING!

THE VET REPOSITORY WAS HIT BY LIGHTNING, AND THE STREETS ARE FULL OF VETS WANDERING LOOSE, LOOKING TO GIVE ANNUAL SHOTS.

RAESIDE
I'LL WAIT UNTIL THEY'RE ROUNDED UP.

PHARMACY
RAESIDE
HERE ARE YOUR ANTI-DEPRESSANTS, ALTHOUGH PERSONALLY, I FEEL A GOOD FACE-LICKING CAN DO THE JOB JUST AS WELL.

FIRST YOU TORE THROUGH THE PUDDLES IN THE BACK-YARD...

THEN YOU WADED THROUGH A MUDDY DITCH...

AND TO TOP IT OFF, YOU FOUND A DEER CARCASS TO ROLL IN!

RAESIDE
IT WAS A SPA DAY.

KIRBY IS SUPPOSED TO BE A HUNTING DOG, BUT SO FAR, HE HASN'T HUNTED ANYTHING.
RAESIDE
I'M A VEGETARIAN.

HEY, BUTCH THE POLICE DOG! STILL RIDING AROUND IN THE BACK OF POLICE CARS?

NOPE, I'VE GONE UNDER THE COVERS.
DON'T YOU MEAN UNDER-COVER?

FOR THE LAST TIME, BUTCH, NO, YOU ARE NOT ALLOWED TO SLEEP IN THE BED!

IF DOGS ADVERTISED PHARMACEUTICALS:
IT'S A SUPER-THIN PILL AND COLORED PINK, SO IT'S EASY TO HIDE UNDER YOUR TONGUE.

CYCLING CHAMPION BUTCH FLETCHER HAS PICKED UP ANOTHER CORPORATE ENDORSEMENT.

BIG DEAL, SO HE CAN BIKE UP A HILL. I'M AN AGILITY COURSE CHAMPION.

BUT DO YOU SEE PIPE MANUFACTURERS AND "TILTING BOARD OF DOOM" BUILDERS SPONSOR ME?

HALF THE TIME I DON'T EVEN GET A BRAND-NAME BISCUIT WHEN I FINISH FIRST.

DOGS HAVE AN INCREDIBLY SENSITIVE NOSE...

A DOG'S SENSE OF SMELL IS THOUSANDS OF TIMES MORE POWERFUL THAN A HUMAN'S.
PSSST!

WHAT AN AMAZING ABILITY.
SOMETIMES IT CAN BE A CURSE.

OW!
WHACK!

OW!
WHACK!

SURELY YOU COULD HAVE FOUND A SHORTER STICK.
STICKS HAVE THE RIGHT-OF-WAY.

I JUST HAD A FLEA TREATMENT.
I HAD A FLEA ONCE.

BUT BEFORE I GOT MY FLEA TREATMENT, HE RAN OFF TO JOIN A FLEA CIRCUS.

SAME OLD STORY. HE BECAME A STAR, FELL IN WITH THE WRONG FLEAS, DISHONEST MANAGER, PARTIES, HEAVY DRINKING...

AND?
HE ENDED UP ON A CAT.

the OTHER COAST
RAESIDE
HERE'S A PHOTO OF MY GREAT-UNCLE BOB, WHO WAS A SHIP'S DOG.

"THE BOAT HE WAS ON GOT CAUGHT IN A FIERCE STORM AND SANK."
LULUBELLE IV

"THE ONLY SURVIVOR, BOB MANAGED TO SWIM TO A NEARBY UNINHABITED ISLAND..."

"WHERE HE SURVIVED ON A DIET OF FISH AND COCONUTS."

LUCKILY, AFTER TWO MONTHS ALONE ON THE ISLAND, IT HAPPENED.
HE WAS RESCUED?

"HIS SQUEAKY FOOTBALL WASHED UP ON THE BEACH."

the OTHER COAST
RAESIDE

KOKO, HERE'S A PHOTO OF YOU AS A PUP, WHICH, LIKE EVERYTHING IN THE HOUSE, YOU CHEWED.

"...LIKE MY SLIPPERS..."

"...YOUR BASKET..."

"...THE FRONT DOORMAT."

FORTUNATELY, YOU DIDN'T CHEW ANY-THING OF REAL VALUE.
YOU OBVIOUSLY HAVEN'T LOOKED BEHIND THE COUCH.

the OTHER COAST
RAESIDE

WOW, IT'S SOME KIND OF VEHICLE.

AND IF IT MOVES, IT MUST HAVE A...

AH, THERE IT IS.

the OTHE
IF THAT'S THE WAY YOU WANT IT, ALICE, I'M GOING OUT THERE AND THROWING MYSELF UNDER A DOG!

RAESIDE
STOMP
STOMP

MY WIFE HATES ME. MY MARRIAGE IS OVER. I'VE GOT NOTHING LEFT TO LIVE FOR. GO AHEAD; TEAR ME TO PIECES.

WELL?

Y'KNOW, IT'S PROBABLY JUST A COMMUNICATION PROBLEM. YOU SHOULD BOTH SEE A MARRIAGE COUNSELOR.

I PICKED THE WRONG DOG.

I THOUGHT YOU TWO WERE GETTING A DIVORCE.
WE DECIDED TO STAY TOGETHER FOR THE SAKE OF THE DOGS.

OOH, A STICK.

THIS IS THE MOST PERFECT STICK IN THE WORLD. THE RIGHT LENGTH, RIGHT WEIGHT, RIGHT TASTE...

OOH, A STICK.

SO MUCH FOR STICK LOYALTY.
WHAT, YOU'VE NEVER TRADED IN A CAR BEFORE?

HOLLYWOOD IS MOURNING THE PASSING OF BIG JIM, THE MOVIE STUNT DOG.

"A VETERAN OF OVER 20 MOVIES, BIG JIM PASSED AWAY AT AGE 15. THAT'S 105 IN DOG YEARS."

"ALL DAY, FOLKS HAVE BEEN COMING BY HIS KENNEL TO LEAVE TREATS AT A MEMORIAL..."

AND AT NIGHT, DOGS ARE COMING BY TO EAT THEM.
HE WOULD HAVE WANTED THAT.

THE DISADVANTAGE TO HAVING A DOCKED TAIL
I FEEL SO TOTALLY OUT OF THIS CONVERSATION.
RAESIDE

RAESIDE
HOW COME YOUR DAD NEVER THROWS A BALL FOR YOU?
HIS HANDS ARE TOO BUSY HOLDING A COFFEE CUP.

PLANS ARE STILL ON TRACK FOR THE FIRST MANNED MISSION TO MARS.

IT'S EXPECTED THE JOURNEY COULD TAKE BETWEEN SIX AND EIGHT MONTHS.

RAESIDE
I WONDER WHY IT'LL TAKE THEM SO LONG TO GET THERE.
I GUESS THEY STOP ALONG THE WAY TO SNIFF ASTEROIDS.

HEY, CHERRY BLOSSOM, MY NAME IS SAKURA, WHICH IS JAPANESE FOR CHERRY BLOSSOM.

BUT THE DIFFERENCE IS I CAN RUN, JUMP AND DO CUTE TRICKS.

WHEREAS YOU JUST SIT THERE AND DO NOTHING.

EXCEPT NOBODY COMPLAINS WHEN I SHED.
RAESIDE

RAESIDE

WHY IS IT WHEN DOGS GATHER, THEY POINTLESSLY MILL AROUND EACH OTHER?
YOU THINK IT'S POINTLESS MILLING, BUT IT'S ACTUALLY CHOREOGRAPHED MILLING.

I WANT YOU TO STAY ON THAT MAT UNTIL YOU DRY OFF.

RAESIDE

"MISSION CREEP."

RAESIDE
SNIFF SNIFF

HURRY UP, KOKO. WE DON'T HAVE ALL DAY!

DOES IT TAKE YOU THAT LONG TO READ A MESSAGE?
IT WASN'T A MESSAGE. IT WAS A NOVEL.

RAESIDE
MISSING
REWARD!
HEY, THAT'S THE POSTER FROM WHEN I GOT LOST IN THE PARK LAST MONTH.

MISSING
REWARD!
BUT I DON'T LOOK ANYTHING LIKE THAT. MY SNOUT ISN'T THAT BIG, AND MY EARS ARE STRAIGHTER.
PHOTOS ON MISSING-DOG POSTERS ARE THE DOG EQUIVALENT OF DRIVER'S LICENSE PHOTOS.

OOH, A STICK!

BUT IT'S IN THE MIDDLE OF THE PATH. IT MIGHT HAVE BEEN DROPPED BY ANOTHER DOG.

RAESIDE
I'LL GIVE IT THE SNIFF TEST...

IT'S ONLY LIGHTLY SLOBBERED, SO IT'S ACCEPTABLE.

HEY, YOU'RE SUPPOSED TO BITE THAT BANK ROBBER!
SORRY, CHIEF. I GOT CAUGHT UP IN THE EXCITEMENT.

SO I GOT TEMPORARILY REASSIGNED TO BASKET DUTY BACK AT THE STATION FOR TWO WEEKS.

BUT I'M STILL ON FULL TUMMY RUBS AND BISCUITS.

CHEZ HOUND
SORRY FOR THE WAIT. THE CHEF TOOK YOUR MEALS OUTSIDE AND BURIED THEM SOMEWHERE.
RAESIDE

RAESIDE
PICK UP AFTER YOUR DOG

YEOW!

YIKES! YOU'VE GOT A PIECE OF GLASS IN YOUR PAW.

THEY SHOULD PUT UP "PICK UP AFTER YOURSELF" SIGNS.

I READ SOMEWHERE THAT ALLIGATORS ARE NATURE'S MOST EFFICIENT PREDATORS.

THEY CAN STAY MOTIONLESS FOR HOURS, WAITING FOR THE OPPORTUNITY TO SCARF A SNACK.

SIMILAR TO THESE TWO.
BUT WOULD YOU LET AN ALLIGATOR SLEEP ON YOUR BED?

"AFTER BEING LOST ON MT. McNASTY FOR SEVEN DAYS, A HIKER AND HIS DOG WERE FOUND BY A SEARCH AND RESCUE TEAM."

"HUGO, THE TEAM'S RESCUE DOG, FOUND THE PAIR AS THE DOG WAS DOWN TO HIS LAST BISCUIT."

A SCUFFLE BROKE OUT BETWEEN HUGO AND THE HIKER'S DOG OVER THE BISCUIT.

THE HIKER IS RECOVERING IN HOSPITAL. HUGO IS RECOVERING AT THE VET.

DOG DESIGNATED DRIVERS:

IT'S NOT FAIR. I NEVER GET TO STICK MY HEAD OUT THE WINDOW AND DROOL.

RAESIDE
OK, KOKO, OPEN-MOUTH CHECK...

AND UNDER-THE-TONGUE CHECK...

WELL, I GUESS YOU ACTUALLY SWALLOWED THE PILL THIS TIME.

COMPARED TO A DOG, HOUDINI WAS AN AMATEUR.
P-TOO!

RAESIDE

COME ON, KOKO! LET'S GO!

REALLY, I DON'T KNOW WHAT YOU FIND SO FASCINATING AT EVERY FIRE HYDRANT.
THEY'RE A DARN SIGHT MORE INTERESTING THAN YOUR FACEBOOK POSTS.

SAKURA, OFF! NO DOGS ALLOWED ON THE COUCH!

RAESIDE
HEY, HOW COME YOU'RE ALLOWED ON THE COUCH?
I'M GRANDFATHERED.

HEY, BUTCH THE POLICE DOG!

NOT ANYMORE. AFTER YEARS OF FAITHFUL SERVICE, THEY RETIRED ME. SAID I WAS TOO OLD.

OK, BUTCH, I THINK IT'S TIME YOU HANDED IN YOUR VEST.
RAESIDE

HERE'S A PHOTO OF MY GREAT-UNCLE CURLY, WHO LIVED IN ENGLAND.

"HE GREW UP IN AN OLD MANOR HOUSE, SURROUNDED BY LUXURY."

WHAT KIND OF LUXURY?

"THE BUTLER WOULD SCUFF UP HIS DOG BED."
RAESIDE

IT'S LIGHTLY BRAISED FILET STEAK IN AN ITALIAN BALSAMIC AND RED WINE REDUCTION, ACCOMPANIED WITH... AH, WHY DO I BOTHER? YOU'RE GOING TO SCARF IT DOWN IN FIVE SECONDS.
RAESIDE

the OTHER COAST
RAESIDE

HEH, ANOTHER COMPUTER HAS BEATEN ANOTHER CHESS GRAND MASTER.

COMPUTERS JUST KEEP GETTING SMARTER. I WONDER WHAT WOULD HAPPEN IF YOU PUT A DOG UP AGAINST A COMPUTER?

THAT'S SILLY. THERE'S NO WAY A DOG CAN OUTSMART A COMPUTER.

IT FAILED THE WADING IN A MUDDY DITCH CHALLENGE.

the OTHER COAST
Z

RAESIDE
TWITCH

TWITCH TWITCH
TWITCH

TWITCH
TWITCH
TWITCH
TWITCH
TWITCH

TWITCH

WALK?
ARE YOU KIDDING? I'M EXHAUSTED.

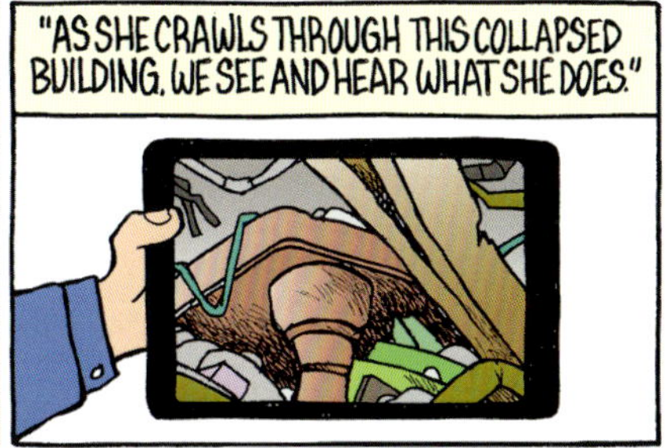

"A COUCH..."

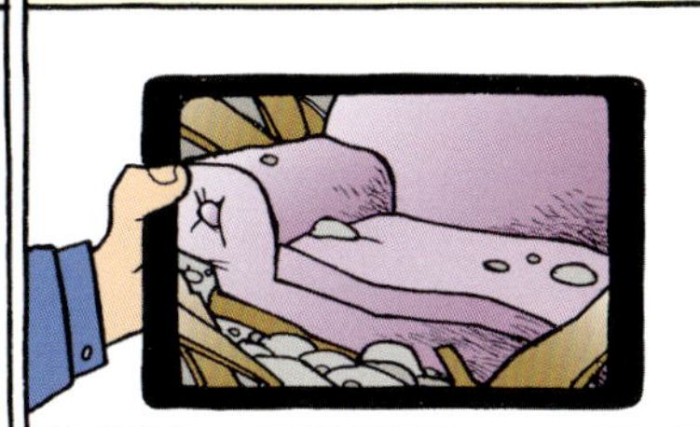

IF DOGS RAN THE PET FOOD COMPANIES...

SNIFF

I ALWAYS LIKE A GOOD-NIGHT SNIFF BEFORE GOING TO BED.

SAKURA, DO YOU BELIEVE IN REINCARNATION?
YOU BET I DO.

IN A PREVIOUS LIFE, I WAS A WOLF RUNNING WITH A PACK IN THE NORTHERN WILDERNESS.

I LIVED BY MY WITS AND CUNNING AND WAS A CHAMPION MOUSE HUNTER.

MOUSE HUNTER?
I WAS A SMALL WOLF.

I'M GOING TO TEACH LOUIE HERE HOW TO SURF.

NO-O-O-O-O-O-!!

SHARK?
LOUIE.
HEY, I LIKE TO CHEW STUFF.

I JUST BOUGHT A BUNCH OF TICKETS FOR TONIGHT'S LOTTERY DRAW. YOU SHOULD GET SOME, TOO. THE JACKPOT IS HUGE!
THANKS, BUT I NEVER PLAY THE LOTTERY.
RAESIDE

I REALLY DON'T LIKE GAMES OF CHANCE.
YOU TOOK A CHANCE ON ME THAT DAY YOU SAW ME IN THE POUND.

REX, I KNOW HOW MUCH YOU LOVE FETCHING THE NEWSPAPER EVERY MORNING. BUT I'VE DROPPED HOME DELIVERY BECAUSE I'VE SUBSCRIBED TO THE DIGITAL EDITION.
RAESIDE

AND WHAT SEEMS TO BE THE PROBLEM WITH REX?
INJURIES SUSTAINED IN A FIGHT TO THE DEATH WITH A MAN-EATING BENGAL TIGER.

RAESIDE
WORMS.
BUT THEY'RE REALLY BIG WORMS.

RUSTY WAS COMPLETELY UNAWARE LUELLA WAS TRYING TO POISON HIM...
OOOH... CHOCOLATES.
CHOCOLATES
RAESIDE

HELLO-O-O, GORGEOUS, MY NAME'S PETE.
OH, PLEASE, YOU'RE A JUNKYARD DOG. YOU DON'T SERIOUSLY THINK I'D HAVE ANYTHING TO DO WITH YOU.

RAESIDE
I WON'T ALWAYS BE A JUNKYARD DOG! IN MY SPARE TIME, I'M TAKING STICK-RETRIEVING AND FRISBEE-CATCHING CLASSES.

I HEARD THAT CHLOE THE SPOKESDOG WAS FIRED.
RAESIDE

"A DOG FOOD COMMERCIAL WENT HORRIBLY WRONG."

AREN'T YOU GOING TO EAT IT?
BUT IT STINKS.

SHE WAS FIRED FOR NOT EATING IT?
SHE WAS FIRED FOR ROLLING IN IT.

I KNOW IT'S HERE SOMEWHERE. I SAW IT FALL.

AH, YES, THERE IT IS!

RAESIDE
YOU JUST SPENT FIVE MINUTES LOOKING FOR A TOAST CRUMB. HOW POINTLESS IS THAT?
IT'S THE THRILL OF THE CHASE.

WHACK! GRUNT
WHACK! GRUNT

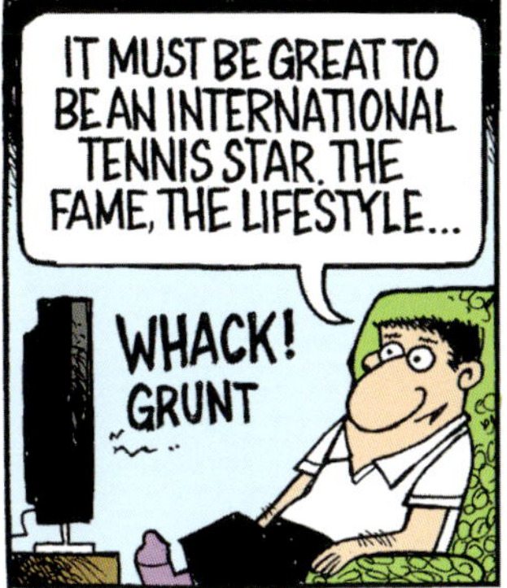
IT MUST BE GREAT TO BE AN INTERNATIONAL TENNIS STAR. THE FAME, THE LIFESTYLE...
WHACK!
GRUNT

THEY GET BIG MONEY FOR PLAYING TOURNAMENTS, CHAUFFEURED LIMOS. SOME EVEN HAVE PRIVATE JETS.
WHACK!
GRUNT

RAESIDE
I CAN CATCH A BALL BETTER THAN THEY CAN, AND ALL I GET IS A DOG DISH WITH MY NAME ON IT.

DON'T PULL MY EAR.
DON'T PULL MY EAR.
DON'T PULL MY EAR.
DON'T PULL MY EAR.
RAESIDE

DON'T BITE HIM.
DON'T BITE HIM.
DON'T BITE HIM.
DON'T BITE HIM.

YOU HAVE SUCH A GENTLE NATURE.
IT'S ACTUALLY CALLED INCREDIBLE SELF-CONTROL.

RAESIDE
THE FOLLOWING IS A TEST OF THE EMERGENCY DOGCAST SYSTEM.

BARK BARK BARK BARK!

IF THIS HAD BEEN A REAL EMERGENCY, LIKE A BURGLAR OR A FIRE, YOU WOULD HAVE BEEN DIRECTED AS TO WHAT TO DO.

WE NOW RETURN YOU TO YOUR REGULARLY SCHEDULED DAY.

I HEAR BARKING IN MY HEAD.
RAESIDE

SOME SCIENTISTS THEORIZE THAT ALL LIFE CAME FROM COSMIC DUST.
RAESIDE

JUST THINK, BILLIONS OF YEARS AGO, WE WERE JUST PARTICLES FLOATING IN THE VASTNESS OF SPACE.

I HOPE MY PARTICLES WERE PUREBRED.

RAESIDE
A DOG CAN HAVE LOTS OF DADS, BUT ONLY ONE MOM.

AS USUAL, CELEBRITY ALLY WHISKYBREATH ARRIVED AT THE AWARDS CEREMONY WITH HER DOG, SALLY.

BUT ORGANIZERS WERE MINDFUL OF LAST YEAR'S AWARDS, WHEN SHE RAN UP ON STAGE AND BEGAN HOWLING.

SO SHE WAS DENIED ENTRANCE TO THE AUDITORIUM.

RAESIDE
HOWEVER, THEY LET HER DOG IN.

RAESIDE

LAST NIGHT, I WAS DOING MY USUAL TURNING AROUND BEFORE LYING DOWN, WHEN SUDDENLY I COULDN'T REMEMBER IF I WAS TO GO CLOCKWISE OR COUNTERCLOCKWISE.
IT'S NO FUN GETTING OLD, BUBBA.

A-A-A...
CHOO!

I'M ALLERGIC TO YOUR DOG.

A-A-A...
CHOO!

RAESIDE
HE'S ALLERGIC TO YOUR PERFUME.

ARTICLE ON NICE FOLKS WHO RESCUE DOOMED DOGS FROM SHELTERS AND RELOCATE THEM TO FOREVER HOMES.

"PRIVATE PILOTS DONATE THEIR TIME AND GAS TO FLY THEM TO THEIR NEW HOMES."
RAESIDE

PACKED INTO CRATES, THEY MUST BE SO CRAMPED IN THOSE PLANES.
I BET THEY HAVE MORE LEGROOM THAN YOU DO WHEN YOU FLY.

MOM TOLD ME NOT TO DATE MIXED BREEDS, AS THEY MIGHT HAVE FLEAS.
OH, I'M VERY FLEA-FREE.

RAESIDE

SCRATCH!
SCRATCH!
SCRATCH!

IT'S ONLY ONE FLEA, AND HE'S VERY OLD. HE'LL PROBABLY BE DEAD BY OUR FIRST DATE!

TURN MY HEAD SIDEWAYS AND PUT ON MY PUZZLED LOOK...

NOW ROLL MY EYES, PIN MY EARS BACK AND SLUMP DOWN ON MY DOG BED.

RAESIDE
YOU DON'T UNDERSTAND A WORD I'M SAYING, DO YOU, KOKO?
I ACTUALLY DO, BUT I DON'T WANT TO SET A PRECEDENT.

RAESIDE
I TRIED BEING A DOG WHISPERER, BUT I COULDN'T GET CLOSE TO THEIR HEADS.

MENTALLY?
PHYSICALLY. I COULDN'T STAND THE DOGGY BREATH.

YOU KNOW ONE OF THE WORST THINGS ABOUT HAVING A DOCKED TAIL?
NO. WHAT IS IT?

NOT BEING ABLE TO KEEP MY NOSE WARM WHEN I CURL UP.
YOU CAN ALWAYS SHARE MY TAIL USING THE BUDDY SYSTEM.
RAESIDE

RAESIDE
JINGLE
JINGLE

WAKE UP, SAKURA. WE'RE GOING FOR A CAR RIDE!
WHAT MAKES YOU THINK THAT?

I HEARD THE CAR KEYS JINGLING.
THAT WAS WIND CHIMES.

GREAT. SO EVERY TIME THERE'S A BREEZE, I'LL AUTOMATICALLY RUN IN CIRCLES, BARKING MY HEAD OFF.

RAESIDE

DO YOU THINK EITHER OF US ARE CLEVER ENOUGH TO FIGURE THIS OUT?
I GUESS I COULD CLIMB OVER YOU.

HERE'S A PHOTO OF MY COUSIN ANDRE, THE SWISS MOUNTAIN RESCUE DOG.
RAESIDE

"HE'D GO OUT LOOKING FOR LOST SKIERS WITH A CASK OF BRANDY AROUND HIS NECK."

WHAT A REWARDING CAREER.
ONLY FOR A SHORT PERIOD.

"HE WAS FIRED AFTER HE BIT A SKIER."
THIS IS A '96. COULD YOU GO GET A '95?

RAESIDE
BARK?

BARK BARK
BARK
YAP YAP
GRRRR
BARK

BARK?

I'M MODERATING A DEBATE.
BARK
BARK ARF
YAP YAP
BARK

RAESIDE
HOV LANE
2 PERSONS OR 2 DOGS

RAESIDE
TRUCKING

HOW COME YOU DIDN'T BARK AT THAT DOG AT THE STOPLIGHT?
I'M A TRUCK DOG. HE'S ONLY A CAR DOG. HE'S NOT BARKWORTHY.

the OTHER COAST
RAESIDE
OOH, A MUDDY DITCH.

"MUDDY DITCHES WERE PUT ON THIS EARTH JUST FOR DOGS TO WADE IN."

"BUT THEN I'LL TRACK MOST OF THAT DITCH BACK INTO THE HOUSE WITH ME."

"AND WHEN MOM SEES THE STAINS ON THE CARPET, I'LL GET A SCOLDING."

"AND FOR THE NEXT HALF HOUR I'LL BE IN THE PROVERBIAL 'DOG HOUSE.'"

HEY, A SCOLDING AND 30 MINUTES OF DIRTY LOOKS IS A SMALL PRICE TO PAY FOR THE JOY OF A DITCH-WADE!

the OTHER COAST
RAESIDE
HAVE YOU EVER WONDERED WHAT WE LOOKED LIKE BEFORE WE EVOLVED?
WHY? MY BREED WAS PERFECT RIGHT OUT OF THE GATE.

"OF COURSE MY ANCESTORS LOOKED JUST LIKE ME AND WERE SKILLED HUNTERS..."

"FIERCE WARRIORS, THEY RELIED ON STEALTH AND CUNNING TO PROVIDE FOR THE PACK."
ANY GAME THAT WANDERS THIS WAY WON'T STAND A CHANCE.

OK, I'LL PASS ON THIS ONE.

NOPE. PASS.

SO, BASICALLY, THEY STARVED.
THEY DID RELY A LOT ON TAKE-OUT.

the OTHER COAST
AUTO SALES
GOOD CHOICE, SIR. THIS BABY IS LOADED.
IT HAS EVERYTHING YOU WANT IN A CAR. LEATHER SEATS, REAR-VIEW CAMERA, ABS, BLUETOOTH, POWER SEATS, PARK ASSIST...
DVD PLAYER, INTERNET, GPS, CD, SATELLITE RADIO, FOG LIGHTS, KEYLESS ENTRY, PUSH-BUTTON START... BASICALLY, IT COMES WITH EVERTHING.
DOES IT COME WITH A DOG?
UH, NO.
SO IT DOESN'T ACTUALLY COME WITH EVERYTHING.

the OTHER COAST
WAIT HERE, SAKURA. I WON'T BE GONE LONG.
YOU TWO HAVE A GOOD SHOPPING TRIP?
YEP, WE SAW LOTS OF COOL STUFF.
ALL I SAW WERE FEET.

SHEEP GPS:
BARK! BARK! BARK!

THE IDITAROD:
TEN DAYS OF MY DOG TEAM RUNNING IN FRONT OF ME. IT WAS AWESOME!

TEN DAYS STARING AT THE HAIRY BEHIND OF THE DOG IN FRONT OF ME. IT WAS HORRIBLE!

LIBRARY

I'D LIKE TO TAKE THIS BOOK OUT.
NO, YOU CAN'T. GIVE IT BACK RIGHT NOW.
QUIET!

BUT I ONLY WANT TO BORROW IT FOR A FEW DAYS.
NO. ALL THESE BOOKS ARE MINE! MINE! MINE! MINE!
QUIET!

BIG MISTAKE TO GIVE AN ALPHA DOG THE JOB OF LIBRARIAN.

I'M THINKING OF GETTING A DOG BUT NOT SURE WHAT KIND.
WHATEVER YOU GET, MAKE SURE YOU GET ONE FROM AN ANIMAL SHELTER.

KOKO CAME FROM A SHELTER, AND HE SETTLED IN TO THE HOUSEHOLD RIGHT AWAY.

RAESIDE
I'VE ALWAYS BEEN SO GLAD I PICKED HIM OUT.
ACTUALLY, I PICKED YOU OUT.

PeRfuMe
COUNTER
RAESIDE
...AND THIS ONE SMELLS LIKE WET DOG. BUT THEN, THEY ALL SMELL LIKE WET DOG.

RAESIDE

OK, THAT'S FAR ENOUGH. LET'S GO HOME.

BUT WE'RE GOING TO MISS THE BEST SNIFFING SPOTS!

OH, REX,
I HAVE A
SURPRISE FOR YOU...

A PUPPY
TO KEEP YOU
COMPANY!

ISN'T HE CUTE?
HE'S EVEN GOT THAT
NEW-PUPPY SMELL.

I HATE
THAT NEW-
PUPPY
SMELL.
IT'S THE
SMELL OF
REPLACEMENT.

USEFUL AGILITY
TRAINING:
OK, I WANT YOU
TO PRACTICE JUMPING
FROM THE BACK SEAT
TO THE DRIVER'S SEAT.

BECAUSE OF
MY PEDIGREE,
I COULD HAVE
BEEN A
SHOW DOG.

BUT ONE OF
MY TEETH IS
CROOKED, SO
I'M NOT SHOW
QUALITY.

GEE, YOU MUST
HAVE BEEN
DISAPPOINTED.
ARE YOU KIDDING? IF IT
WASN'T FOR THAT TOOTH,
I'D HAVE TO ENDURE BEING
PUT IN A STUFFY TRAVEL
CRATE AND DRAGGED AROUND
ENDLESS DOG SHOWS.

RAESIDE

THAT SQUIRREL ESCAPED UP A TREE AGAIN?
TREES ARE IN COLLUSION WITH SQUIRRELS.

RAESIDE
DESPITE THE FACT WE CONSIDER THE ACCUSED INCREDIBLY GUILTY, HE GAVE US THE "SAD EYES" LOOK, SO WE'RE ACQUITTING HIM.

RAESIDE

THAT'S NOT TAKING A DOG FOR A WALK. THAT'S TAKING A DOG FOR A DRAG.
THERE'S NOT EVEN TIME TO SNIFF ANYTHING ON THE WAY.

RAESIDE
IT'S A NEW DOG FOOD. FOUR OUT OF FIVE VETS RECOMMEND IT.

I GUESS THE FIFTH VET ACTUALLY TASTED IT.

DON'T MISS THIS WEEKEND, WHEN WE SHOW EVERY SUPERMAN MOVIE BACK TO BACK.

I'D LOVE TO BE ABLE TO FLY LIKE SUPERMAN. WIND ON MY FACE, AIR RUSHING PAST MY EARS.

DOGS CAN FLY.

"EVERY TIME WE STICK OUR HEADS OUT THE CAR WINDOW."
RAESIDE

A LOW-PRESSURE SYSTEM WILL MOVE INTO THE AREA TOMORROW...
L

BRINGING WITH IT A 90% CHANCE OF SHOWERS...

AND A 90% CHANCE OF WET DOG.
RAESIDE
WITH A 90% CHANCE OF MUDDY PAW PRINTS ON THE CARPET.
MAKE THAT 100%.

OBEDIENCE CLASS RECESS BELL:
SQUIRREL!
STAY SIT
RAESIDE

WHEN I SAW THIS ADORABLE DOG COAT, I JUST HAD TO BUY IT FOR CLEO. I THINK SHE FEELS QUITE SMART IN IT.
I FEEL LIKE I'M IN A SAUNA.
RAESIDE

THE STEVE FURY WILDLIFE HOUR
THE GRACEFUL GAZELLE DRINKS AT THE WATER HOLE...

BUT LOOK. A LION HAS QUIETLY SNUCK UP ON THE UNSUSPECTING GAZELLE AND IS ABOUT TO POUNCE.

DON'T JUST STAND THERE, STEVE! DO SOMETHING! SHOUT! WAVE YOUR ARMS! THROW THE CAMERA!

IN ONE SWIFT MOTION, THE GAZELLE IS DOWN.
ANOTHER GAZELLE SACRIFICED FOR RATINGS.

I HEARD THAT CHANCE, THE LAB DOWN THE STREET, HAS PASSED AWAY.

UNDERSTANDABLY, HER OWNER IS DEVASTATED OVER HER LOSS.

BUT YOU KNOW WHAT SHE DID? SHE WENT OUT AND RESCUED ANOTHER DOG FROM A SHELTER.

RAESIDE
THAT'S GOOD. IT WOULD BE A SHAME TO WASTE A NICE PERSON.

I SEE A CLOUD THAT LOOKS LIKE A PONY WITH A LONG TAIL.
RAESIDE

I SEE A MAGNIFICENT CASTLE WITH LONG COLORFUL PENNANTS FLYING FROM TALL TURRETS, A MOAT AND A SWEEPING LAWN.

IS THERE A DOG ON THE LAWN?

NO.
THEN IT'S NOT THAT MAGNIFICENT.

WHAT A DAY. I'VE BEEN WORKING LIKE A DOG.

RAESIDE

LET ME REPHRASE THAT.
I'VE BEEN DREAMING ABOUT CHASING SQUIRRELS. THAT'S HARD WORK.

RAESIDE
BARRY, HOW DID YOUR OBEDIENCE CLASS GO?
LOUSY. ALL THE DOGS EXCEPT ME GRADUATED.

I HAD ACED "SIT," "STAY" AND "HEEL."

SO WHY DIDN'T YOU GRADUATE?
I FAILED "SHAKE A PAW."

RAESIDE
KOKO, YOU ALWAYS WALK WITH YOUR HEAD DOWN.

SURELY THE GROUND CAN'T BE THAT INTERESTING.
IT'S A LOT MORE INTERESTING THAN A PHONE.

RAESIDE
MY DOG IS AN OBEDIENCE CLASS GRADUATE
MY DOG ISN'T

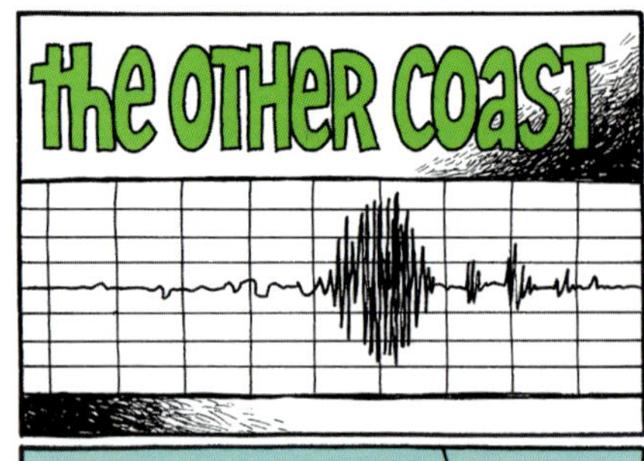
the OTHER COAST

RAESIDE
THIS IS INTERESTING. IT SAYS HERE ANIMALS CAN PREDICT AN EARTHQUAKE.

I FIND IT HARD TO BELIEVE THEY'RE BETTER THAN US AT PREDICTING EARTHQUAKES.

EARTHQUAKE! QUICK, GET TO AN EMERGENCY SHELTER!

MERGENCY
SHELTER

the OTHER COAST
RAESIDE

HELLO. MOM HAS PLANTED A VEGETABLE GARDEN.

MMM, LOOK AT ALL THAT LOVELY MOIST SOIL.

OOH, AND I CAN SMELL MANURE!

MUST! RESIST! TEMPTATION!

A FRESHLY DUG GARDEN IS DOG CATNIP.

the OTHER COAST

RAESIDE

CHOMP!

CHOMP!

CHEW CHEW

CHEW

URP!

WATCHING YOU EAT IS LIKE WATCHING A SWARM OF LOCUSTS.

DO THEY COME WITH GRAVY?

HEY, SOMEONE HAS LEFT THEIR BALL BEHIND.

IT'S ALONE IN THE WORLD, EXPOSED TO THE ELEMENTS AND FEELING ABANDONED.

RAESIDE

A RESCUED BALL ALWAYS TASTES BETTER THAN A STORE-BOUGHT BALL.

MY NAME IS BIG PETE. I'M PART HUSKY, PART WOLF.

RAESIDE
SNATCH

BUT MOSTLY WOLF.

RAESIDE
THAT'S BOBBY. HE'S INTO CHASING BICYCLES.
SO?

NEXT THING HE'LL BE CHASING CARS, THEN PICKUP TRUCKS, THEN MOTOR HOMES, SEMI TRUCKS, ETC....

BICYCLES ARE A GATEWAY CHASE.

RAESIDE

THE BACK-FEET SCUFF.

THE FOUR-PAWS SCUFF.

AND THE SCRABBLE -AND-KNEAD.

IT'S EXHAUSTING MAKING THE BED EVERY NIGHT.

RAESIDE
THAT GUY HAS A DOG.
HOW CAN YOU TELL?

THERE'S SLOBBER ON HIS BACK WINDOWS.

RAESIDE
SORRY TO BE SO LATE, KOKO. I HOPE YOU'RE NOT ANGRY WITH ME.
YOU BET I AM! YOU DIDN'T TAKE ME WITH YOU!

BUT YOU'RE WAGGING YOUR TAIL, SO I'M OBVIOUSLY FORGIVEN.
NO, YOU'RE NOT! THIS IS A CASE OF THE TAIL WAGGING THE DOG.

HEY, SAM, WHAT'RE YOU UP TO?
NOT MUCH.

WHY IS YOUR VOICE SO HOARSE?
COLLAR IS TOO TIGHT. IT HASN'T BEEN LOOSENED IN YEARS.

SOME PEOPLE SHOULD HAVE TO TAKE AN APTITUDE TEST BEFORE THEY'RE ALLOWED TO HAVE A DOG.
THEY IGNORE MY COLLAR, YET THEY'LL BUY THEMSELVES A NEW OUTFIT EVERY FEW MONTHS.
RAESIDE

RAESIDE
THE LADDER OF DESPAIR...

TILTING BOARD OF DOOM...

TUNNEL OF NO RETURN...

THE THINGS WE DOGS DO FOR A DOG BISCUIT.
SAD, ISN'T IT?
1
2
3

MISSING
REWARD

MISSING
REWARD

THERE'S NOTHING SADDER THAN A FADED AND TATTERED MISSING-PET POSTER.

BREED?
PUREBRED LAB.
DOG LICENSES

OH, AND SOME BORDER COLLIE.
DOG LICENSES

OK, AND A BIT OF POODLE, SHEPHERD AND DALMATIAN.
DOG LICENSES

MUTT.
WE PREFER "MIXED BREED."
DOG LICENSES

BERNIE, YOU STILL WORKING FOR A PARK RANGER?
I'VE BEEN SENT AWAY FOR SENSITIVITY TRAINING.

"WE WERE ON PATROL LOOKING FOR POACHERS."

"WHEN I CAME ACROSS A DEER CARCASS..."

I ROLLED IN IT.
I WAS GOING TO COMPLIMENT YOU ON YOUR NEW COLOGNE.

GOOD GIRL, LASSIE! YOU SAVED THOSE NUNS FROM THAT ABANDONED MINE!

THAT LASSIE IS SUCH A FAKE. SHE RUNS FOR MILES THROUGH THE WOODS TO GET HELP...

AND NOT ONCE HAS SHE EVER PAUSED TO CHASE A SQUIRREL UP A TREE.
RAESIDE

LASSIE IS A TV STAR. TV STARS DON'T CHASE SQUIRRELS.
YOU'RE RIGHT. SHE HAS ASSISTANTS WHO CHASE THEM FOR HER.

RAESIDE
OOH, THIS SMELLS INTERES...

C'MON, MAX, WE DON'T HAVE ALL DAY!
URK!

HOW MANY TIMES HAVE I WAITED PATIENTLY OUTSIDE A DEPARTMENT STORE WHILE YOU WERE INSIDE CHECKING OUT DIFFERENT PERFUMES?

FOLLOWING THE MAJOR EARTHQUAKE, COUNTRIES AROUND THE WORLD OFFERED HELP...

"INCLUDING A SEARCH AND RESCUE TEAM FROM HERE, ALONG WITH THEIR RESCUE DOG, SCOUT."

"SCOUT'S JOB WILL BE TO LOOK FOR PEOPLE TRAPPED IN THE DEBRIS."

I HOPE SCOUT IS ALSO LOOKING FOR TRAPPED PETS.

AWWW, KOKO IS GIVING ME THE "ADORING LOOK."

HOW SWEET. YOU'RE HERE TO KEEP ME COMPANY.

OOPS.

YOU WEREN'T JUST KEEPING ME COMPANY, YOU WERE SCROUNGING.
DOGS MULTITASK.

I LOVE DOGS. I'VE BEEN AROUND THEM ALL MY LIFE.

THUNDER THUNDER THUND
INCOMING!

SLAM!

HE KNOWS A DOG PERSON USUALLY KEEPS A BISCUIT IN THEIR POCKET.

CITY POUND

I WANT TO GO ON ONE OF THOSE.
NO, YOU DON'T.
RAESIDE

"YOU'D BE PUT IN A TINY CRATE AND STUFFED IN THE HOLD, ALONG WITH THE BAGGAGE."

HOWEVER, AS I AM A SMALL DOG, I WILL TRAVEL IN THE MAIN CABIN WITH THE OTHER PASSENGERS.

WOW, LUCKY YOU.
ARE YOU KIDDING? HAVE YOU EVER TASTED AIRLINE FOOD?

THE BREEDER ASSURED ME HE'D ONLY GROW TO BE MIDSIZED...
RAESIDE

OOH, MOM HAS PLANTED A NEW FLOWER BED.
RAESIDE

LOOK AT ALL THOSE LOVELY SOFT FLOWERS I COULD LIE ON.

BUT IF MOM CATCHES ME CRUSHING HER FLOWERS, I'LL CATCH HECK.

HEY, IF THEY DON'T WANT DOGS TO LIE ON THEIR FLOWERS, THEY SHOULDN'T CALL THEM FLOWER BEDS.

RAESIDE
OH, SURE, HE MAY BE A HIGHLY TRAINED POLICE DOG, SKILLED IN CATCHING BAD GUYS AND TRACKING DOWN LOST KIDS, BUT I'M THE DOG WHO'S SITTING IN THE FRONT SEAT.

YIKES! CHECK OUT THAT UNDERBITE!

AND THAT IS ONE SERIOUS OVERBITE!

THESE UGLY DOG CONTESTS ARE HILARIOUS.
HOW ABOUT AN UGLY PET-OWNER CONTEST?
RAESIDE

LOOK AT KOKO. HE'S NOT A DOG, HE'S A COUCH POTATO.

HARD TO IMAGINE HE'S RELATED TO WORKING DOGS, LIKE SEARCH AND RESCUE DOGS.

EVEN LASSIE THE TV DOG WOULD GO OUT OF HER WAY TO RESCUE KIDS WHO FELL INTO WELLS.
RAESIDE

IF YOU FELL BEHIND THE COUCH CUSHIONS, I'D RESCUE YOU.

HEY, MICK. I'D LIKE TO TRY MY PAW AT HERDING SHEEP.
YOU? A TINY TERRIER? DON'T MAKE ME LAUGH!

THAT'S JUST BLATANT BREEDISM! DENYING ME EMPLOYMENT BECAUSE OF MY BREED!
ALL RIGHT, ALL RIGHT. GIVE IT A SHOT.

RAESIDE
I THINK I'VE GOT A FLEA.

RAESIDE
BARK! BARK!

BARK! BARK! BARK! BARK!

I'M FOCUS TESTING A NEW BARK.

RAESIDE

THAT'S JERRY. HE USED TO BE A BIG STAR ON THE DOG AGILITY CIRCUIT. HE EVEN HAD DOG FOOD SPONSORS.

BUT THEN THEY FOUND PERFORMANCE-ENHANCING LIVER TREATS IN HIS KENNEL.

NOW HE JUST DOES STUPID PET TRICKS FOR DOG BISCUITS.
I THINK I'VE SEEN HIM IN DOG SHAMING PHOTOS.

RAESIDE
THE MORNING RUSH HOUR.

LOOK. SAKURA, I BOUGHT YOU A NEW TOY.
RAESIDE

OH, SURE, YOU THINK I'M SO SIMPLE-MINDED, MY FRIENDSHIP CAN BE BOUGHT WITH A CHEAP, TAWDRY STUFFED TOY.

AND IT'S A SQUEAKY TOY.

IT MAY BE CHEAP AND TAWDRY, BUT THE SQUEAK DOES GIVE IT SOME CLASS.

OH, LOOK. A DEAD FISH HAS WASHED ASHORE.

POOR LITTLE GUY. I WONDER WHAT HAPPENED TO HIM.

WAS HE TRAPPED IN AN OXYGENLESS DEAD ZONE? A VICTIM OF RISING OCEAN TEMPERATURES? MAYBE HE SWAM INTO AN ALGAE BLOOM.

RAESIDE
PHEW! I THOUGHT THAT MARINE BIOLOGY LECTURE WOULD NEVER END.

the OTHER COAST
BAR
COCKTAILS
OK, GENTLEMEN, BAR IS CLOSED. TIME TO GO HOME.
C'MON, GUYS, YOU CAN'T STAY HERE ALL NIGHT.
HERE WE GO AGAIN.
URP!
WHO WANTS TO GO FOR A CAR RIDE TO THE VET?
JINGLE
NEVER FAILS.

the OTHER COAST
MONTY! HERE, BOY!
MONTY!
MONTY!
MO-O-NTY!
THERE YOU ARE. I GUESS YOU DIDN'T HEAR ME CALLING.
I THINK HE'S GOING DEAF.
I JUST PRETEND TO BE DEAF SO I GET ME MORE SNIFFING TIME.

the OTHER COAST
DOG, AFTER MONTHS OF CHASING ME, I GET THE FEELING YOU DON'T REALLY WANT TO CATCH ME.
IN FACT, YOU ONLY CHASE ME SO YOU'LL HAVE SOMETHING TO DREAM ABOUT WHEN YOU'RE SLEEPING.
HUH. THAT'S JUST CRAZY SQUIRREL TALK.

THIS AFTERNOON, AS TEMPERATURES SOARED, A DOG WAS FOUND INSIDE A LOCKED CAR.

POLICE BROKE A WINDOW AND REMOVED THE DOG, BUT IT WAS TOO LATE TO SAVE HER.

EVERY SUMMER, THIS HAPPENS. DON'T PEOPLE EVER LEARN?
THEY SHOULD BE TESTED FOR THE "MORON GENE" BEFORE THEY'RE ALLOWED TO TAKE A DOG HOME.
RAESIDE

RAESIDE
I HATE TAKING A NEW BALL TO THE DOG PARK, WHERE EVERY DOG IS WAITING FOR ME TO DROP IT.

I GOT A POSTCARD FROM COUSIN HERB, WHO'S A BEACH DOG IN MEXICO.

A BEACH DOG? WOW. TROPICAL SUNSETS, WARM SAND. HOW ROMANTIC!
OH, IT'S NOT THAT ROMANTIC.

SUNGLASSES? FLIP-FLOPS? WATCHES?
RAESIDE

BROOM!
EEK! THUNDER!

I GOTTA FIND A PLACE TO HIDE FROM THE EVIL THUNDER!

YOU COULDN'T JUST HIDE BEHIND THE CHAIR?
THAT'S THE FIRST PLACE THUNDER LOOKS.

A LAWN BEING WATERED DURING A DROUGHT. I'LL CALL THE CITY.

OK, YOU CAN CALL THE CITY NOW.

I DON'T WANT YOU SITTING ON THIS PLANT, KOKO.
ROGER THAT.

UMM, WHAT AM I NOT SUPPOSED TO DO AGAIN? OH, RIGHT, SIT ON SOMETHING. PROBABLY THE BED, OR THE COUCH.

OR THE DRIVER'S SEAT IN THE CAR? I SHOULD CHASE A SQUIRREL BEFORE DINNER... LOOK, A NEW PLANT!

THE ADVANTAGE OF HAVING A SHORT ATTENTION SPAN.

IMPORTANT MILESTONES IN A PUPPY'S LIFE:
THE EAR TATTOO

SPAYING OR NEUTERING
RAESIDE

DISCOVERING THE COUCH
DON'T EVEN THINK ABOUT IT!

DISCOVERING THAT YOUR MOM WILL EVENTUALLY GIVE UP IF YOU'RE PERSISTENT ENOUGH.

UH-OH. THIS COULD BE TROUBLE.

BARK.

RAESIDE

IT'S NOT THE VOLUME, IT'S THE DELIVERY.

BOY, WILL I BE GLAD WHEN THIS HEAT WAVE IS OVER.

"I JUST FOUND TWO SQUIRRELS COOLING OFF IN MY WATER BOWL."

OOH. SO YOU POUNCED ON THEM?
RAESIDE
NAH. I CAN'T THINK OF ANYTHING MORE UNAPPETIZING THAN SOGGY SQUIRREL.

PEOPLE MARK THE PASSAGE OF TIME IN YEARS. HOW DO DOGS MARK IT?
I THINK IT'S IN THE NUMBER OF TAIL WAGS.

BUT WHAT IF YOU'RE AN ABANDONED DOG LANGUISHING IN A SHELTER? NOT MUCH TAIL-WAGGING THERE.

I GUESS THEY MAKE UP FOR IT WHEN THEY'RE RESCUED.
A WHOLE LOT OF WAGGING TO CATCH UP ON!
RAESIDE

RAESIDE

AWW. HOW SWEET. DOG KISSES.

OWW! THAT'S NOT A KISS, THAT'S A NIBBLE!

BUT IT WAS A LOVE NIBBLE.

RAESIDE
POSITIVELY
NO DOGS
ALLOWED IN STORE

WITH THAT KIND OF ATTITUDE, I WOULDN'T WANT TO GO IN THERE ANYWAY.

HERE I AM, FAITHFULLY GUARDING MY DAD'S CAR.

RAESIDE

BARK! BARK! BARK! BARK!

SOMEONE ENTERED THE THREE-FOOT EXCLUSION ZONE.

MEANWHILE, AT NASA:
OK, I'VE RIGOROUSLY TESTED OUR LATEST SUPER-STRONG CARBON-FIBER MATERIAL...

"I DID EVERYTHING TO IT, INCLUDING SHOOTING IT AND TRYING TO CRUSH IT."

IT PASSED EVERY TEST EXCEPT THE LAST ONE.
WHICH WAS?

"I GAVE IT TO MY DOG TO PLAY WITH."
RAESIDE

BOB, YOUR PHONE IS RINGING.

THAT RING TONE SOUNDS WAY TOO CLOSE TO THE SOUND OF CAR KEYS JINGLING.
RAESIDE

DECODING A DOG'S TAIL:
THE I'M SO HAPPY TO SEE YOU, I COULD BURST, TAIL

THE I DON'T KNOW YOU, SO I'M BEING COOL TOWARDS YOU, TAIL.
ONE WAG

THE YEAH, IT'S OK TO PAT ME, TAIL.
THE I HEARD THE WORD "VET," TAIL.

MARATHON ROUTE

THERE ARE A WHOLE BUNCH OF FOLKS OUTSIDE RUNNING.
MUST HAVE SEEN A SQUIRREL.

REALLY? YOU THINK SO?
WHY ELSE WOULD ANYONE RUN?

ALL OF THEM CHASING ONE SQUIRREL?
THEY PROBABLY EACH HAVE THEIR OWN SQUIRREL.

HEY, A FIRE HYDRANT. CAN WE STOP SO I CAN CHECK MY MESSAGES?

LOOK, THERE ARE MY BUDDIES. CAN WE GO OVER AND SAY HELLO?

SQUIRRELS! A PACK OF THEM AND THEY'RE TAUNTING ME!

I PREFER WALKS. YOU CAN'T DO ANYTHING ON RUNS.

RAESIDE

SO WHERE DID THE PHRASE "WORKING LIKE A DOG" COME FROM?
MUST BE AN OXYMORON.

RAESIDE
THE AIRCRAFT IS NOW READY FOR BOARDING. WE WILL BE BOARDING PUREBREDS FIRST, FOLLOWED BY MIXED BREEDS AND MUTTS.

LOOK AT THOSE LEFTOVER TOAST CRUMBS.

I'LL PUT THEM OUTSIDE FOR THE BIRDS.

I THOUGHT I HAD FIRST RIGHT OF REFUSAL ON TOAST CRUMBS.
RAESIDE

RAESIDE
THERE'S VINNIE. POOR GUY HAS HIS TAIL DOCKED AND EARS CROPPED.

I DON'T KNOW WHAT POSSESSES PEOPLE TO RUIN A PERFECTLY GOOD DOG.

HEY, PETE, THE GUYS WANT TO KNOW HOW COME YOU ALWAYS GET THE FRONT SEAT.
DOG WALKING

RAESIDE
MY DAD PAYS EXTRA FOR THE FRONT SEAT.
DOG WALKING

C'MON, REX, OPEN THE DOOR! THIS SAUNA IS OVER 140 DEGREES, AND I'M BOILING IN HERE!
RAESIDE
NOW YOU KNOW WHAT IT'S LIKE WHEN YOU LEAVE ME LOCKED INSIDE THE CAR ON A HOT DAY.

the OTHER COAST

RAESIDE

CLUNK
CLUNK

SOME CITY WORKERS HAVE TURNED UP WITH A CHAIN SAW.

BRRR...
BRRR...

AND THEY'RE CUTTING DOWN THAT OLD TREE ACROSS THE STREET.

BZAWW!

THAT'S YOUR FAVORITE TREE, ISN'T IT, KOKO?

CRASH!

I GUESS YOU'RE A BIT UPSET IT'S BEEN CUT DOWN.

DARN RIGHT I AM! HOW WOULD YOU LIKE IT IF SOMEONE TOOK A CHAIN SAW TO YOUR BATHROOM?

the OTHER COAST
BANK

HAH! BUTCH HAS PICKED UP HIS TRAIL. HE'LL BE IN HANDCUFFS IN NO TIME.

HEY, THIS SMELLS LIKE TEX, THE GUY WHO ALWAYS GIVES ME A DOG BISCUIT EVERY TIME HE SEES ME.

IF I TRACK HIM DOWN AND HE'S ARRESTED, I WON'T GET ANY MORE DOG BISCUITS.

RAESIDE
BUT I HAVE A JOB TO DO, PUTTING BANK ROBBERS BEHIND BARS.

THAT'S TOO BAD YOU LOST HIM. I WAS SURE YOU WERE HOT ON HIS TRAIL.

the OTHER COAST
RAESIDE

NO DOGS ALLOWED ON BEACH

NO DOGS ALLOWED IN POOL AREA

PARK RULES NO DOGS IN PONDS!

NO DOGS IN FOUNTAIN

BEATS ME WHY THEY CALL THESE THE DOG DAYS OF SUMMER.
MAYBE IT'S BECAUSE THEY SPEND THE DAY FINDING NEW PLACES WHERE DOGS CAN'T GO.

WHY THERE ARE NO DRIVE-THRUS FOR DOGS:
PICKUP WINDOW
RAESIDE

WHAT BREED IS YOUR DOG?
NO IDEA. JOEY'S A RESCUE.

HOW OLD IS HE?
YOUR GUESS IS AS GOOD AS MINE.

AND HE ONLY HAS THREE LEGS?
YUP.
RAESIDE

IT DOESN'T SLOW HIM DOWN?
HE DOESN'T REALIZE HE HAS THREE LEGS.

BUS LANE
RAESIDE

HOV LANE

BIKE LANE

IT SEEMS EVERYONE GETS THEIR OWN LANE THESE DAYS.
EXCEPT DOG WALKERS.

MY LITTLE DOG, FRANKIE, TURNED UP AT THE HOUSE COVERED IN MUD AND REEKING OF YUCK.

HE'D OBVIOUSLY BEEN WADING IN MUDDY DITCHES AND ROLLING IN A DEER CARCASS.
RAESIDE

BECAUSE HE WAS HANGING OUT WITH YOUR DOG.
I'M MENTORING FRANKIE.

A MAN AND HIS DOG OUT FOR THEIR MORNING WALK DISCOVERED A BODY IN A ROADSIDE DITCH.

YIKES, IT MUST BE SO TRAUMATIC TO UNEXPECTEDLY COME ACROSS A CORPSE.

IT'S THE FLASHBACKS, DOC... I CAN'T SLEEP. NO APPETITE. EVEN MY SQUEAKY BALL IRRITATES ME...
RAESIDE

IF WE SHAME DOGS FOR DOING WHAT COMES NATURALLY TO THEM, WHY NOT WILDLIFE?
ME AND THE PACK SNUCK UP ON A SHEEP AND ATE IT.

RAESIDE
I ATE A COW.
(THE WIFE KILLED IT, BUT I ATE IT.)

I TRAMPLED A CIRCUS TRAINER!
AND IT FELT GOOD.

I BIT A SURFER I THOUGHT WAS A SEAL.

BARK
BARK
BARK
THAT SOUNDS LIKE KOKO BARKING AT ANOTHER DOG.

I WONDER IF BARKS DIFFER BY COUNTRY. WOULD A FRENCH DOG UNDERSTAND A SPANISH DOG?

BARKING MUST BE A UNIVERSAL LANGUAGE ALL DOGS UNDERSTAND.

WHICH IS WHY, UNLIKE PEOPLE, DOGS GET ALONG WITH EACH OTHER.
RAESIDE

RAESIDE
Y'KNOW, I THINK I'D MAKE A REALLY GOOD ZOMBIE.

"I'D HAVE A COMBINATION OF SMALL-DOG ATTITUDE AND ZOMBIE."
RRRRRR

"I'D BE SO FEARSOME PEOPLE WOULD FLEE BEFORE ME."
RRRRRR.

BUT IF EVERYONE FLEES, YOU WOULDN'T BE ABLE TO EAT THEIR BRAINS.
AS A PUREBRED ZOMBIE, I'D ONLY EAT CANNED, GOURMET BRAINS.

KOKO, I'VE JUST GOT A JOB AS A SNIFFER DOG.

WOW, WHAT ARE YOU SNIFFING FOR? DRUGS? EXPLOSIVES? CRIMINALS?

RAESIDE

NOT BED BUGS?
YUP.

FITNESS CLUB
RAESIDE

IS THERE ANYTHING BETTER THAN A BRISK WALK ON A TREADMILL?
WALKING A DOG AT AN ANIMAL SHELTER?
AND THERE'S NO MEMBERSHIP FEE.

SHE DOESN'T LOOK LIKE MUCH - HALF A TAIL, RAGGEDY EARS, MISSING TEETH - BUT SHE'S SMART AS A WHIP AND HAS A GENTLE PERSONALITY.

RAESIDE
WHAT A GREAT LITTLE DOG.
WHICH GOES TO SHOW ONE SHOULDN'T JUDGE A DOG BY ITS COVER.

BARK!
BARK!

BARK!
BARK!

RAESIDE
BARK!
QUIET, KOKO!

ONLY A TRUE DOG OWNER CAN RECOGNIZE THEIR DOG'S BARK.

A GANG OF STREET THUGS ATTACKED A BLIND MAN OUTSIDE THE BUS STATION...

KNOCKING HIM TO THE GROUND, WHERE THEY TOOK HIS WALLET.

HOW COULD ANYONE BE SO CRUEL AND HEARTLESS?

RAESIDE
THEY'RE ANIMALS.
HEY, NO ANIMAL WOULD EVER DO ANYTHING LIKE THAT.

THAT LOOKS LIKE A DRIED-UP PEA FROM SUNDAY'S DINNER.

AND THAT GRAVY STAIN WOULD BE FROM LAST WEEK'S BEEF STEW.

KOKO, MUST YOU KEEP NOSING AROUND ON THE FLOOR?
RAESIDE
IT'S NOT NOSING, IT'S DOG ARCHAEOLOGY.

RAESIDE

IT USED TO BE PEOPLE TOOK THEIR DOGS OUT FOR A MORNING WALK
NOW THEY TAKE THEIR PHONES OUT FOR A MORNING WALK.

I'M TIRED OF WAKING UP IN THE MIDDLE OF THE NIGHT TO FIND LEO HERE LYING ON THE BED.

SO I BUILT HIM HIS OWN DOGHOUSE TO SLEEP IN OUTSIDE. HE'S GOING TO USE IT TONIGHT.

RAESIDE

AFTER SERVING IN AFGHANISTAN, I WAS HAVING A HARD TIME ADJUSTING, UNTIL I SAW SHEP IN THE CITY POUND.

HE'S BEEN A REAL LIFESAVER.
DITTO.
RAESIDE

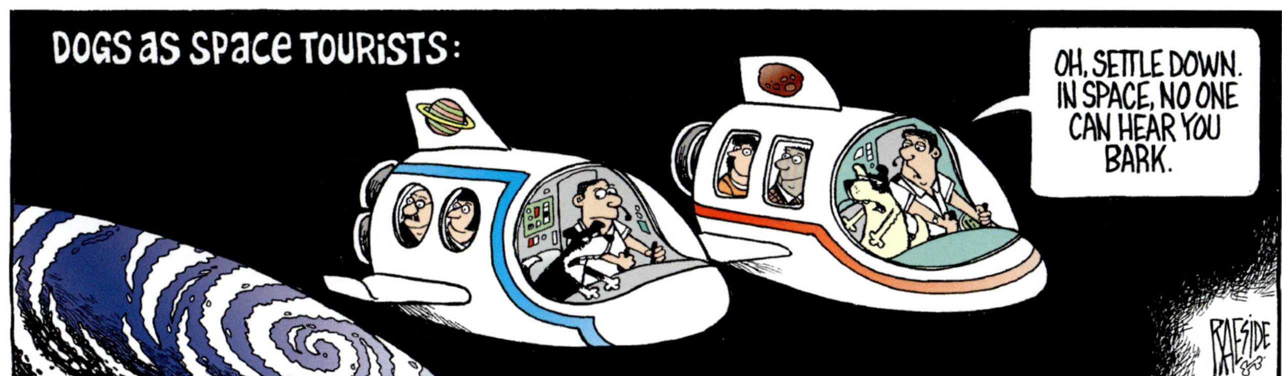
DOGS AS SPACE TOURISTS:
OH, SETTLE DOWN. IN SPACE, NO ONE CAN HEAR YOU BARK.
RAESIDE

FOR DOGS, THERE ARE TWO TYPES OF DELIVERY PEOPLE:
THOSE WHO CARRY DOG BISCUITS IN THEIR POCKETS...
...AND THOSE WHO DON'T.
RAESIDE

I WONDER IF THAT PLANE CARRIES A DOG RESCUED FROM A FOREIGN COUNTRY.

RAESIDE
OR PERHAPS IT'S CARRYING A SHIPMENT OF SQUEAKY TOYS.

THAT'S A BIT SELFISH. WHAT COULD BE MORE IMPORTANT THAN A RESCUED DOG?
RESCUED SQUEAKY TOYS?

OOH, TOAST! DROP IT, MOM. DROP IT. DROP IT.

RAESIDE
DROP IT. DROP IT. DROP IT. DROP IT. DROP IT. DROP IT.

OOPS! I DROPPED IT.
SCARF!

A GOOD BORDER COLLIE CAN CONTROL MORE THAN JUST SHEEP.

BARK! BARK!
RAESIDE

OOO... PERHAPS I SHOULDN'T HAVE SAID THAT.

BARK WOOF BARK YAP YAP YAP YAP BARK GRRR WOOF BARK!!

YOU REALLY SHOULD LEARN TO FILTER YOUR BARKS.

THE MYSTERY OF MISSING MOBSTER KNUCKLES MALONE HAS BEEN SOLVED.

HIS BODY WAS DISCOVERED IN NEARBY WOODS BY A MAN OUT WALKING HIS DOG.

OH, COME ON! HE DIDN'T FIND IT! HIS DOG DID!

A CLASSIC EXAMPLE OF SLOPPY JOURNALISM.

I KNOW YOU'RE OUT THERE, DOG.
RAESIDE

THAT'S RIGHT. I KNOW YOU'RE HIDING BEHIND MY TREE.

YOU'RE WASTING YOUR TIME. YOU'RE NOT FOOLING ANYONE.

I CAN HEAR YOUR TAIL WAGGING.
NEXT TIME, I'M TAPING UP MY TAIL.

The Other Coast

?

UH-OH. FLAGGING ON A TREE ISN'T A GOOD SIGN...

THE PARKS DEPARTMENT HAVE TIED FLAGGING AROUND THAT TREE, SO THE TREE FALLERS KNOW THIS IS THE TREE TO BE CUT DOWN.

RAESIDE

The Other Coast
RAESIDE

IT'S TOO HOT TO DO ANYTHING TODAY EXCEPT FLOP UNDER A SHADY TREE.

SQUIRREL!

BARK BARK BARK

SQUIRREL CHASING BY PROXY.
BARK
BARK

the OTHER coast
NO, YOU'RE NOT COMING AND THAT'S FINAL.

I'D LIKE TO TAKE YOU TO THE MALL WITH ME, BUT IT'S TOO HOT OUT THERE.

"EVEN WITH THE WINDOWS CRACKED, TEMPERATURES INSIDE THE CAR WOULD SOAR."

"CONCERNED PASSERS-BY WOULD SEE YOU IN DISTRESS AND BREAK A WINDOW TO SAVE YOU."

"I'D END UP ON THE EVENING NEWS, AND PROBABLY HAVE TO PAY A HEFTY FINE."

THAT'S RIGHT, THIS IDIOT LEFT HIS DOGS IN THE CAR IN THESE TEMPERATURES!

DURING A HEATWAVE, I PREFER THAT YOU STAY AT HOME.
YET THIS WASN'T AN ISSUE YESTERDAY, WHEN YOU DROVE US TO THE VET TO GET OUR ANNUAL SHOTS.

the OTHER coast
I BET I'D HAVE MADE A GREAT PIRATE MASCOT.
PIRATES

AWRIGHT, ME HEARTIES. PREPARE TO ENGAGE THAT SPANISH GALLEON!

WHAT?

OH, COME ON! COULDN'T YOU HAVE GONE WHEN WE WERE ASHORE BURYING TREASURE?

ARR BILLY

AT WHICH POINT YOU WOULD BE TRADED FOR A PARROT.
PIRATES

OH, DARN! I'VE LOST THE BEST PIECE OF MEAT.

REMEMBER THE FIVE-SECOND RULE. IF YOU CAN RETRIEVE IT OFF THE FLOOR IN FIVE SECONDS, YOU CAN EAT IT.

SWOOP!

RAESIDE
BEAT YOU BY 3 SECONDS.

A SEARCH AND RESCUE OPERATION IS HAPPENING ON MT. McNASTY...

YOU FOUND THE LOST SKIER? GOOD BOY! HERE'S YOUR DOG BISCUIT.

BUT, UMM... WHERE IS HE? DIDN'T YOU RESCUE HIM?
NOPE.

YOU FOUND HIM, BUT YOU DIDN'T RESCUE HIM?
SEARCHING IS ONE BISCUIT, RESCUING IS TWO.

WOW, A HOLLYWOOD MOVIE THAT COST 500 MILLION TO MAKE HAS FLOPPED AT THE BOX OFFICE. I WONDER WHY.
HOLLYWOOD

WERE THERE ANY DOGS IN THE MOVIE?

RAESIDE
NO.
THERE'S YOUR REASON.
HOLLYWOOD

ACCORDING TO THIS, IN ONLY A FEW YEARS' TIME, WE'LL BE ABLE TO BUY DRIVERLESS CARS.
DRIVING

WHO THE HECK WOULD WANT A DRIVERLESS CAR?
DRIVING

RAESIDE
WOOF2

RAESIDE
DOG WALKING
ON A RAINY DAY, A VAN FULL OF WET DOGS HAS ITS OWN TROPICAL MICROCLIMATE.

I HEAR THEY MAY BE LOOKING FOR A NEW ACTOR TO PLAY JAMES BOND.
RAESIDE
IT SHOULD BE A DOG.

A DOG 007?
WHY NOT? THERE ARE TONS OF DOGS ON TV, AND A CAT WAS IN THE MOVIE "YOU ONLY LIVE TWICE."

BUT THE CAT DIDN'T DO ANYTHING.
MY POINT EXACTLY. DOGS ARE ALL NOISE AND ACTION.

SO, ANNOYING AND INCESSANT BARKING WILL STOP AN EVIL VILLAIN FROM WORLD DOMINATION?
UNLESS HE HAS A TREAT IN HIS POCKET.

DOG BOOK CLUBS:

WE WERE GOING TO READ "WUTHERING HEIGHTS," BUT RUSTY HERE CHEWED OUR ONLY COPY.
RAESIDE

THIS IS MOLLY. SHE'S OUR RESCUE DOG.
RAESIDE

SHE SURE REMINDS ME OF MY OLD DOG, TESS. BOY, I MISS HER.

DID I MENTION MOLLY'S ALSO A THERAPY DOG?
SOMEONE NEEDS A HUG.

SAKURA, HAVE YOU EVER WONDERED IF THERE IS A PARALLEL WORLD OUT THERE?
A WHAT?

YOU KNOW, A PLANET OF SIMILAR SIZE WITH OCEANS, CONTINENTS, MOUNTAINS...

BESIDES ANIMALS, BIRDS AND FISH, THERE WOULD, OF COURSE, BE PEOPLE.

BUT WOULD THEY BE MORE ADVANCED THAN US?
IF THEY HAVE OUTLAWED PUPPY MILLS, DEFINITELY, YES.
RAESIDE

I'M THE TOP DOG HERE!
NO, YOU AREN'T. I'M TOP DOG HERE!
RAESIDE

BARK!

OK, OK, I GIVE UP! YOU WIN!
IF ONLY OUR ELECTION CAMPAIGNS WERE THAT QUICK.

CAFÉ
I LIKE TO TAKE MY COFFEE OUTSIDE WITH KOKO TIED TO THE TABLE TO KEEP ME COMPANY.

OH, LOOK. A SQUIRREL.

RAESIDE

OOH, A HYDRANT. LET'S SEE WHAT EVERYONE'S TALKING ABOUT.

RAESIDE

HOW TYPICAL. THE CONVERSATION DEGENERATES INTO MINDLESS BARKING.

the OTHER COAST
RAESIDE
KOKO, IF YOU COULD GO BACK IN TIME, WHAT WOULD YOU DO?

THAT'S EASY. I'D GO BACK AND CHANGE THINGS TO MAKE THE WORLD A BETTER PLACE.
LIKE WHAT?

"I'D STOP WORLD LEADERS FROM SQUABBLING, PREVENTING FUTURE WARS."

"I'D SAVE SPECIES FROM EXTINCTION."

"AND I'D INITIATE THE FIRST RECYCLING PROGRAM."

SO WHAT WOULD YOU DO IF YOU COULD GO BACK IN TIME?
I'D HAVE A SECOND DINNER.

the OTHER COAST
ZZZZZZZZZZZZZZZZZZZZZZZZZZ

RAESIDE
ZZZZZZZZZZZZZZZ

ZZZZZZZZZZZZZZZZZZ

ZZZZZZZZZZ

SNAP!

YOU CAN'T TELL THE DIFFERENCE BETWEEN A BLACK FLY AND A YELLOW-STRIPED WASP?
CUT ME SOME SLACK. I'M COLORBLIND.

the OTHER COAST
RAESIDE

GUESS WHAT, SAKURA, I HAVE AN ANCESTOR WHO WAS A PIRATE DOG!
PIRATES

"HE SAILED WITH LEGENDARY PIRATE CAPTAIN, LARRY DESPICABLE, IN THE ARR BILLY."
ARR BILLY

"DESPICABLE AMASSED A FORTUNE IN TREASURE, BUT NONE OF IT HAS EVER BEEN FOUND."

WELL, THIS CLEARS UP THE MYSTERY OF THE MISSING TREASURE.
PIRATES

SO, YOU'RE TELLING US YOU BURIED ALL THE TREASURE, BUT CAN'T REMEMBER WHERE?

the OTHER COAST

RAESIDE

SNIFF
SNIFF SNIFF

SNIFF SNIFF
SNIFF SNIFF

SNIFF SNIFF SNIFF
SNIFF SNIFF
SNIFF

WELL, THAT WAS A GOOD DAY.
IF YOU CAN CALL INHALING DIRTY LAUNDRY AND STOLEN HOTEL BATHROOM AMENITIES A GOOD DAY.

...AND THE RIBBON FOR BEST IN BREED GOES TO PEACHES WOO WOO AND HER HANDLER, DEBBIE.

DOG SHOWS ARE SO SHALLOW. THEY'RE BASICALLY JUST CANINE BEAUTY CONTESTS.
RAESIDE

WHY CAN'T THERE BE A SHOW THAT GOES BEYOND THE PRIMPING AND PREENING, AND FOCUSES INSTEAD ON THE INNER DOG?

YES! LIKE A SMARTEST DOG CONTEST.
I WAS THINKING MORE OF A BED HOGGING COMPETITION.

RAESIDE
THIS HAS TO BE THE FINEST PRIZE TO HAVE FALLEN INTO MY PAWS!

I MUST BE ALERT. THERE ARE THOSE WHO WOULD WANT TO RELIEVE ME OF IT.

AND WHAT'S THIS APPEARING OVER THE HORIZON? A THREAT OF MASSIVE PROPORTIONS!

SAKURA, IF YOU'RE NOT GOING TO CHEW THAT BONE, IT'S GOING IN THE GARBAGE.
SAIL ANY CLOSER, AND YOU'LL GET YOUR ANKLE BITTEN.

OH, GOODY! WE'RE TURNING IN TO THE MALL PARKING LOT.

WE'RE SLOWING DOWN, PULLING INTO A PARKING SPACE. ENGINE OFF...

DRIVER'S SEAT, HERE I COME!
RAESIDE

WOULD IT KILL YOU TO WAIT UNTIL I ACTUALLY GET OUT OF THE CAR?
ACTUALLY, YES, IT WOULD.

FIRST, I'LL SNACK ON A COUPLE OF POTATO CHIPS.
RUSTLE RUSTLE

THEN GET THE SPAGHETTI READY TO COOK.
RUSTLE RUSTLE
RAESIDE

OH, AND I SHOULD FEED THE DOGS.
DOGS
RUSTLE RUSTLE

HOW DID YOU...?
DOG FOOD BAGS HAVE A UNIQUE RUSTLE.

AVALANCHE RESCUE DOG TRAINING:
OK, SCOUT. GO OUT THERE AND FIND LARRY.
RAESIDE

YOU FOUND ME. GOOD WORK, BOY!

IT WOULD MAKE MY JOB EASIER IF SKI OUTFITS WERE BEEF-FLAVORED.

RAESIDE
2016 DOGS CALENDAR

HEY, KOKO, I'M GOING TO BE IN A DOG CALENDAR AS THE DECEMBER DOG.

SO YOU'LL BE WEARING A CHRISTMAS COAT?
UMM.. NO. NO COAT.

OH. IT'S THAT KIND OF CALENDAR.
I'LL STILL BE WEARING MY COLLAR, SO IT'S TASTEFUL.

Z

OK, I'VE DONE MY PILATES. NOW, WHEN IS BREAKFAST?

WHAT DO YOU THINK IS THE MOST ADMIRABLE TRAIT IN OUR DOG?

IS IT LOYALITY? COMPANIONSHIP? UNCONDITIONAL LOVE?

ENTHUSIASM? TENACITY? RESILIENCE?
HOW ABOUT PATIENCE?

WE CONTINUE WITH CHILLING PERSONAL TALES OF ALIEN ABDUCTIONS...

I WAS HELPLESS, STRAPPED TO A TABLE WHILE THE ALIENS PROBED ME...

AND WHAT'S WORSE, I'M NOW WALKING AROUND WITH AN ALIEN MICROCHIP IMPLANTED IN ME.

HEY, WE HAVE MICROCHIPS IMPLANTED IN US, BUT YOU DON'T HEAR US COMPLAINING.
CRY-BABY.

RAESIDE
I ATE ONE OF MY MOM'S SHOES

I SNEAK FOOD OFF THE TABLE

I DUNNO WHY THEY CALL IT "DOG SHAMING."
I WOULDN'T BE ASHAMED OF DOING THAT.

RAESIDE

THE FIRST DAY OF THE FALL SQUIRREL-CHASING SEASON.

I'M THE IDEAL MOUNTAIN RESCUE DOG, AS I GREW UP GOING FOR WALKS HERE.

YEP, I KNOW THIS MOUNTAIN LIKE THE BACK OF MY PAW.

SUCCESS!

DID YOU FIND THE LOST SKIER?
NOPE, BUT I FOUND A FRISBEE I LOST FOUR YEARS AGO.
RAESIDE

RAESIDE
the OTHER coast

LOOK, KOKO, THE LEAVES ARE TURNING.

IT'S MOTHER NATURE TELLING US THE SEASON IS CHANGING BY PUTTING ON A COLORFUL DISPLAY.

AS THE TREES SHED THEIR LEAVES, THE GROUND BECOMES A SPECTACULAR CARPET OF YELLOW AND GOLD.

I DON'T RECALL YOU WAXING QUITE SO POETIC WHEN I SHED A FEW HAIRS ON THE CARPET.

the OTHER COAST

RAESIDE
IT'S DEPRESSING TO THINK THAT IN ONLY A FEW SHORT WEEKS, WINTER WILL BE HERE.

SOON, A BLANKET OF SOFT, WHITE FLAKES WILL COVER... WHAT THE..?

IS IT REALLY SNOWING? BUT IT CAN'T BE. IT'S TOO WARM TO SNOW!

HANG ON...SINCE WHEN DO SNOWFLAKES SMELL LIKE BIG PETE?

HEY, BIG PETE, I THINK IT'S TIME YOU WENT TO THE GROOMER!

the OTHER COAST
RAESIDE
OK, I'M GOING TO PARK...
PARK?

BARK!
BARK!
BARK!
BARK!

BARK!
BARK!
BARK!
BARK!

BARK!
BARK!
BARK!
BARK!

...PARK THE CAR IN THE GARAGE.

I WASTED ALL MY HAPPY BARKS FOR NOTHING.

the OTHER COAST
RAESIDE
I FOUND THIS MAGAZINE FROM 1965 THAT PREDICTED WHAT LIFE WOULD BE LIKE IN THE FUTURE.
SCIENCE STUFF

"EVERYONE WOULD HAVE A FLYING CAR."

"WE WOULD HAVE COLONIES ON MARS."

"ROBOTS WOULD DO ALL THE MANUAL TASKS."
I CHANGED THE OIL IN YOUR FLYING CAR AND BAKED YOU A CUPCAKE.

Y'KNOW, ALL THESE THINGS ARE ACTUALLY POSSIBLE, WITH THE EXCEPTION OF ONE PREDICTION...
WHICH IS?

DOGS WOULD BE TRAINED TO STAY OFF THE FURNITURE.
THERE'S ALWAYS ONE CRAZY PREDICTION.

I THINK IN THIS CASE, IT SHOULD BE THE DOG THROWING THE BALL.

OH, BOY! THE FIRST SNOWFALL OF THE SEASON.

THE FIRST LEAP IN THE SNOW OF THE SEASON.

THE FIRST ROLL IN THE SNOW OF THE SEASON.

AND THE FIRST DIRTY LOOK OF THE SEASON.

LOOK, KOKO. I BOUGHT YOU A DRIED PIG'S EAR TO CHEW ON.

WELL? WHAT ARE YOU WAITING FOR?
THE REST OF THE PIG.

AAH, NOTHING LIKE THE MORNING AFTER AN OVERNIGHT SNOWFALL.

A PRISTINE BLANKET OF WHITE, MY WORLD IS AN UNSULLIED BLANK CANVAS.

RAESIDE

GRRRR...
ERK.

I WONDER IF ZOMBIES HAVE DOGS.
IF THEY DO, THERE ARE BOUND TO BE CULINARY CONFLICTS.

RAESIDE
MMMM... CANNED BRAINS.
BUT, BUT... THAT'S MY DOG FOOD!

NICE SNOWMAN, BUT IT'S MISSING SOMETHING.

RAESIDE

HEY, LARRY, NEW DOG?
MAYBE. I SAW THIS LITTLE GUY AT THE SHELTER TODAY.

RAESIDE
I'M TAKING HIM FOR A TEST DRIVE.
ACTUALLY, I'M TAKING HIM FOR A TEST DRIVE.

IN THE SWISS ALPS:
TAKE THAT BRANDY CASK AND FIND THE LOST SKIER!

RAESIDE

WELL?
HE SENT ME BACK FOR CIGARS.

RAESIDE

MOBILE DOG GROOMER
DOGGY2

LISTEN TO THIS, KOKO. THERE'S A HOTEL HERE THAT CLAIMS TO BE VERY DOG-FRIENDLY.
TRAVEL

"EVERY ROOM HAS A DOG BED..."

"THEY EVEN SUPPLY A DOG BOWL AND BISCUIT."
RAESIDE

PRETTY MUCH EVERYTHING YOU'D WANT.
DOES ROOM SERVICE HAVE SQUIRRELS?

YIKES, IT REALLY SNOWED LAST NIGHT.

RAESIDE
BAD MORNING?
COULDN'T FIND MY FIRE HYDRANT.

KOKO, HAVE YOU BEEN CHASING SQUIRRELS AGAIN?
PANT PANT PANT

OH, SURE, IT SEEMS HARMLESS TO CHASE A LITTLE SQUIRREL. BUT IT DOESN'T STOP THERE.
RAESIDE

NEXT THING YOU KNOW, YOU'RE CHASING AFTER BIGGER ANIMALS: DEER, BEARS, ELK, TIGERS, ELEPHANTS...

SQUIRRELS ARE A GATEWAY CHASE.
I CAN QUIT SQUIRRELS ANY TIME I WANT.

the OTHER COAST

ROGER, THE MOUNTAIN RESCUE DOG IS ON A TRAINING COURSE ON MT. McNASTY:

OK, I'VE BURIED ANOTHER TRAINER IN THE SNOW...

GO FIND HIM, ROGER!

NOW HOLD ON, I'M DETECTING A DOUBLE STANDARD HERE.

I GET INTO TROUBLE WHEN I BURY STUFF, BUT IT'S OK WHEN YOU DO IT?

AND IF THAT'S THE CASE, I SEE NO REASON WHY I SHOULD HELP YOU FIND HIM.

OH, FOR PETE'S SAKE... I'LL GO DIG HIM OUT.

HELLO? GETTING SERIOUS HYPOTHERMIA HERE...

IF HE GIVES YOU A BISCUIT, CAN I HAVE IT?

RAESIDE

the other coast
A MOUNTAIN RESCUE TEAM IS TRAINING ON MT. McNASTY THIS AFTERNOON.
IT'S NOT FAIR. THE RESCUE GUY GETS TO GO ON SKIS, BUT THE RESCUE DOG HAS TO WADE THROUGH THE SNOW.
"THERE'S NO REASON WHY RESCUE DOGS CAN'T ALSO BE ON SKIS."
"OR WHY NOT SNOWBOARDS? WE'D LOOK PRETTY COOL ON A RESCUE MISSION."
DOGS COULD EVEN BECOME PART OF THE APRÈS SKI SCENE!
THAT WOULD PROBABLY LEAD TO SOME AWKWARD MOMENTS.
HEY! WHO ATE MY CHEESE FONDUE?

the other coast
RAESIDE
I'M A DACHSHUND. I'M BRED TO DIG OUT BADGERS.
HEY, DO I HAVE A PROPOSITION FOR YOU!
THERE ARE TWO SQUIRRELS LIVING DOWN THAT HOLE. GET IN THERE AND DIG 'EM OUT.
OH? AND WHAT'S IN IT FOR ME?
WELL, I THOUGHT WE COULD SPLIT THE SQUIRRELS 50-50.
OH, YEAH? I'M THE ONE DOING ALL THE DIGGING! I WANT BOTH!
IF IT WASN'T FOR ME, YOU WOULDN'T KNOW THERE WERE SQUIRRELS THERE!
ALL RIGHT, YOU GO DIG THEM OUT!
NO WAY. I'M A HERDING DOG, NOT A DIGGING DOG!
CHIP-MUNKS
THE HUNTING INSTINCT IS TRUMPED BY THE SELFISH GENE.

MEET BUTCH, THE JUNKYARD DOG.
RAESIDE

AS JUNKYARD DOGS GO, BUTCH IS THE TOUGHEST.
I ONCE WRESTLED A GRIZZLY BEAR JUST FOR KICKS.

BUT COME HALLOWEEN NIGHT...
BOOM!
BOOM!

BUTCH BECOMES JUST LIKE EVERY OTHER DOG.

RAESIDE
REX, YOU LOOK SO CUTE WITH THAT BALL.
THROW THE BALL, DAD.

I HAVE TO TAKE A PHOTOGRAPH OF THIS.
THROW THE BALL?

HOLD STILL... OK, GOT IT.
CLICK!
THROW THE BALL? PLEASE?

I'LL POST THIS ON MY FACEBOOK PAGE.
I HATE SMARTPHONES.

THERE IS A PART FOR A DOG IN AN OUTDOOR CATALOG...
TALENT
AGENT

BUT THE PRODUCERS ARE SPECIFICALLY LOOKING FOR A PUREBRED.

RAESIDE
BLATANT MIXEDBREEDISM.

I LOVE THE MORNING AFTER AN OVERNIGHT SNOWFALL. THE WORLD IS FRESH AND NEW.
RAESIDE

THERE ARE NO SCENTS OR SMELLS... I'M THE ONLY DOG IN THE WORLD!

I'M THE ONLY DOG IN THE WORLD!
I'M THE ONLY DOG IN THE WORLD!
I'M THE ONLY DOG IN THE WORLD!

PORTRAIT GALLERY
RAESIDE

WHAT ARE YOU READING?
A MYSTERY NOVEL CALLED "THE CASE OF THE MISSING BISCUIT."

WELL, I CAN ALMOST GUARANTEE HOW IT ENDS. THE SMALL DOG DID IT.

FLIP FLIP FLIP FLIP FLIP

RAESIDE
BY GOLLY, YOU'RE RIGHT. THE SMALL DOG ATE THE BISCUIT.
IT'S ALWAYS THE SMALL DOG.

I DON'T THINK SANTA CLAUS EXISTS.
WHAT?

"THINK ABOUT IT. HE SNEAKS INTO THE HOUSE IN THE MIDDLE OF THE NIGHT."

RAESIDE
AND YET NO DOGS BARK AT HIM. EXPLAIN THAT!
SANTA HAS BARKING EXEMPTION.

RAESIDE
SO, WHAT DO YOU THINK? I CALL IT "SNOWMAN WITH HIS SNOW DOG."

WHY IS HIS DOG WAY OVER THERE?
HE'S AN OFF-LEASH SNOW DOG.

HOLLYWOOD HOWIE. HOW IS THE ACTING CAREER GOING?

RAESIDE
SLOW, KOKO. I'M REDUCED TO DOING BARK-OVERS.

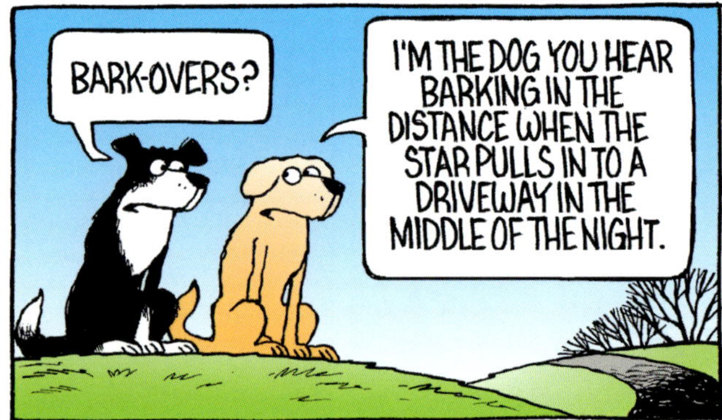
BARK-OVERS?
I'M THE DOG YOU HEAR BARKING IN THE DISTANCE WHEN THE STAR PULLS IN TO A DRIVEWAY IN THE MIDDLE OF THE NIGHT.

RAESIDE

50% OFF
PRE XMAS SALE!

MALL
AND THEY SAY DOGS GO CRAZY WHEN THEY SEE A SQUIRREL.
EXIT
RAESIDE

HEY, IT'S LABRADOR BOB, THE SERVICE DOG.
RAESIDE

I LOVE A DOG IN UNIFORM.

the OTHER COAST
RAESIDE

WOW, THAT IS THE COOLEST SNOW DOG!

THAT'S BECAUSE IT'S A RESCUE SNOW DOG.

the OTHER COAST
RAESIDE

Y'KNOW, THIS REALLY IS A MAGNIFICENT PIECE OF WORK.

THE STRONG FORM, THE UNDERSTATED ELEGANCE...

ART-HATING BARBARIAN!
I LOVE ART, AS LONG AS IT ISN'T IN MY WAY.

The Other Coast
RAESIDE

BRACE YOURSELVES MORTALS, WANDA THE WITCH IS IN TOWN!

THAT'S RIGHT, I'M A CARD-CARRYING, BONA FIDE, MISCHIEF-CAUSING, BROOM-RIDING WITCH!

ONCE THEY GET A TASTE OF MY AWESOME POWERS, THEY WILL FLEE IN TERROR! BWAHAHAHAH!

BOOM!
WHEEEEEEEEEE.....

MOVE OVER, DOG. YOU'RE NOT THE ONLY ONE WHO'S SCARED OF FIREWORKS.

The Other Coast
RAESIDE
AH, THE SIGNS THAT WINTER IS APPROACHING...

TREES SHEDDING THEIR LEAVES.

SQUIRRELS STOCKING THEIR LARDER.

BEARS PREPARING TO HIBERNATE.

OH, AND THERE IS ONE MORE SIGN...

MUDDY PAW-PRINTS ON THE CARPET.

AS A KID, DID YOU EVER WISH FOR IMPOSSIBLE CHRISTMAS GIFTS?
WHEN I WAS 5, I ASKED FOR A REAL, WORKING FIRETRUCK.

WHEN I WAS THE SAME AGE, I ASKED FOR A PINK UNICORN.
I ONCE ASKED FOR A MARTIAN SPACESHIP.

I WONDER IF ANYONE'S IMPOSSIBLE WISH HAS EVER COME TRUE?

RAESIDE
I GOT MY FOREVER HOME.

OOPS, A COOKIE CRUMB FELL ON THE FLOOR.

RAESIDE

THAT WAS PRETTY SLICK, KOKO.
I COME FROM A LONG LINE OF CRUMB-DIVERS.

THE 2016 FIRESTORM XLS. PURE MOTORING PERFECTION FOR THE DISCERNING MOTORIST!

HAVE YOU NOTICED HOW MANY CAR COMMERCIALS HAVE DOGS IN THEM?

IT'S ALMOST LIKE YOU HAVE TO PUT A DOG IN THE CAR TO SELL IT.

RAESIDE
WE'VE BECOME COMMISSIONED SALES DOGS.
WITHOUT THE COMMISSION.

OOH, SNOW. THIS MUST BE THE WHITE CHRISTMAS EVERYONE WAS HOPING FOR.

WHITE CHRISTMA-SES ARE VASTLY OVERRATED.
I'VE LOST ALL FEELING IN MY TAIL.
RAESIDE

HEY, WE SHOULD CHECK OUT THIS NEW MOVIE PLAYING AT THE MULTIPLEX. THE REVIEWER GAVE IT FOUR TAIL WAGS OUT OF FIVE.
ENTERTAINMENT
RAESIDE

WHAT DO YOU THINK OF THIS STEAK?
IT'S A BIT TOUGH TO CHEW...

NOT ONLY IS IT TOUGH, IT TASTES AWFUL.

WHAT A DISAPPOINT-MENT.
IT'S NOT EVEN FIT TO FEED TO A DOG.
I THINK YOU SHOULD LET US MAKE THAT CALL.
RAESIDE

the OTHER COAST
RAESIDE
DOG CLOTHES

easter

SUMMER HOLIDAYS

Halloween
TRICK OR TREAT

CHRISTMAS

WHY DOES EVERY HOLIDAY HAVE TO BE CELEBRATED BY PUTTING SOMETHING GOOFY ON MY HEAD?
WHAT ABOUT THIS PIRATE HAT FOR NEW YEAR'S EVE?

the OTHER COAST
IN THE TEETH OF A BLIZZARD, THE FEARLESS RESCUE DOG GOES INTO ACTION.

RAESIDE
MY MISSION IS TO USE MY KEEN SENSE OF SMELL TO FIND A LOST SKIER.

AS THE SNOW PILES UP, IT'S A RACE AGAINST TIME.

I'M PICKING UP A SCENT HERE...

FOUND HIM!

OK, SO WE DON'T HAVE LOST SKIERS IN THE BACKYARD.

the OTHER COAST
RAESIDE
HELLO? THAT LOOKS LIKE MONEY.

WOW, IT IS! IT'S A TWENTY-DOLLAR BILL! I COULD BUY A LOT OF COOL STUFF WITH THIS.

LIKE A FUR-LINED DOG BED, OR MY OWN PERSONAL COUCH, OR A TRUCK-LOAD OF SOUP BONES, OR A DOG COLLAR MADE OF CHEESE...

OR A SQUIRREL-SHAPED TOY THAT LIGHTS UP AND PLAYS THE THEME FROM "LASSIE" WHEN I CHEW IT...

OR A BATTERY-POWERED SHEEP, OR... UH...UMM...

USE IT TO BUY SQUEAKY TOYS FOR UNDERPRIVILEGED DOGS.

the OTHER COAST
RAESIDE
DO YOU EVER WONDER IF THERE ARE ALIEN BEINGS OUT THERE?

MORE IMPORTANTLY, ARE THERE ALIEN DOGS OUT THERE?

AND IF THERE ARE, WOULD THEY LOOK LIKE US?

CHANCES ARE THEY WOULDN'T, AS THEY WOULD HAVE EVOLVED MILLIONS OF LIGHT-YEARS AWAY FROM US.

BUT I IMAGINE THEY MIGHT SHARE SOME DOGGY TRAITS WITH US.

PHEEUW! OH, THAT JUST REEKS, MAX!
GACK! I CAN'T BREATHE IN THERE!

THE OTHER COAST
CITY POUND
RASIDE
POOR REX HAS BEEN HERE FOR MONTHS. HE SEEMS UNADOPTABLE.
IF ANYONE CAN WORK MIRACLES, IT'S SANTA.

THE OTHER COAST
SANTA'S WORKSHOP
RASIDE
OK, I'M READY TO GO. ALL THE GIFTS ARE WRAPPED...
THE NAUGHTY-AND-NICE LIST HAS BEEN CHECKED TWICE...
THE REINDEER ARE GROOMED AND FED...
A SLEIGH RIDE JUST ISN'T A SLEIGH RIDE WITHOUT A DOG IN THE FRONT SEAT.

the other coast
I HATE THE HOLIDAY SEASON. IT MEANS SPENDING TIME IN A BOARDING KENNEL.
MY UNCLE BENNY ESCAPED FROM A BOARDING KENNEL.
RAESIDE
"HE WAS HEAD OF THE KENNEL ESCAPE COMMITTEE AND PLANNED THE OPERATION."
"IT WAS A CUNNING PLAN: DIG A TUNNEL TO THE PARK OUTSIDE."
"THEY EVEN HID THE EXCAVATED DIRT UNDER THEIR DOG BEDS."
"FINALLY, EARLY ONE MORNING, THE TUNNEL WAS COMPLETED, AND THEY BUSTED OUT."
AND THEY MADE A CLEAN GETAWAY?
NOT REALLY. BY 5 P.M., THEY GOT HUNGRY AND BROKE BACK IN TO THE KENNEL.

I HEAR MOM AND DAD HAVE MADE THEIR NEW YEAR'S RESOLUTIONS.
WHAT'S THAT?
the other coast
IT'S WHEN THEY RESOLVE TO CUT OUT THEIR BAD HABITS IN THE NEW YEAR.
IT WOULD BE LIKE US RESOLVING TO NOT SNEAK ONTO THE BED OR SCARF FOOD OFF THE TABLE.
WHY ON EARTH WOULD WE DO THAT?
WELL, IT WOULD MAKE US BETTER DOGS.
RAESIDE
ALTHOUGH, GIVEN A CHOICE, I'D RATHER CONTINUE SNEAKING ONTO THE BED.
AND SCARFING FOOD OFF THE TABLE IS PART OF DOGGY CULTURE.

RAESIDE
OH, NO! A BUG HAS HIT THE WINDSHIELD.
SPLAT!

GOLLY, IT'S NOT MOVING. I HOPE IT'LL BE OK.

DAD, THERE'S A SQUISHED BUG ON THE WINDSHIELD. DO SOMETHING!
WHIMPER

I WAS THINKING MORE ALONG THE LINES OF CPR.

MEANWHILE, OUTSIDE THE GROCERY STORE:

RAESIDE
SHUFFLE

SHUFFLE SHUFFLE

SHUFFLE
OUT!

I WAS JUST GOING TO HELP MY DAD CARRY OUT THE GROCERIES.

IT'S TIME I FINALLY GOT DOWN TO WRITING THE NOVEL THAT'S BEEN INSIDE ME FOR SO MANY YEARS.

BUT LIKE ALL GREAT NOVELS, IT NEEDS THAT FIRST KILLER SENTENCE TO HOOK THE READER.

RAESIDE
AH, I GOT IT.
Woof.

REALLY? I WOULD HAVE SAID "YAP."
THE HERO IS A BIG DOG, NOT A SMALL DOG.

AND LOOK, UP ON THAT BRANCH! A SQUIRREL!

WE'LL PAUSE TO STARE AT IT FOR A WHILE.

AND STARE AT IT SOME MORE...

KEEP STARING...
DOG WILDLIFE SHOWS ARE SO PREDICTABLE.

RAESIDE
I'VE GOT A JOB AS A HOTEL DOG.

"I HANG AROUND THE LOBBY AND GREET THE GUESTS."

WHEN GUESTS CHECK IN, I CAN TELL WHO IS STRESSED, WHO IS SAD, WHO IS TIRED AND WHO IS A GOOD TIPPER.

"AND WHEN THEY CHECK OUT, I CAN TELL WHO IS MAKING OFF WITH HOTEL TOWELS."

RAESIDE
WHAT A LOVELY PART OF THE WOODS. PERFECT FOR DOG WALKS.

GENERATIONS OF DOGS MUST HAVE ENJOYED WALKING THESE SAME WOODS.

AND THEY STILL ARE.

ALSO BY ADRIAN RAESIDE...

THE RAINBOW BRIDGE: A Visit to Pet Paradise is a magical tale of adventure and a valuable fable for anyone who cherishes the companionship of a family pet.

Seven-year-old Rick and his beloved dog Koko are inseparable. They cavort in the swimming hole, chase each other through the fields, play fetch and wrestle. But their relationship changes as Koko grows old and his health declines.

With Koko's passing, Rick is devastated. But on Christmas Eve he is woken by Buster, a flatulent but well-intentioned messenger dog, who suddenly appears at the boy's bedside. Buster ferries Rick to a magical paradise for pets where Rick is reunited with Koko; it fills Rick's heart with joy. It's a place where cats burrow through fields of catnip, no couch is off-limits to dogs and Frisbees are flung endlessly. This mysterious adventure is truly a holiday miracle!

Adrian Raeside captures the special bond between humans and their pets, and with marvellous illustrations, brings a gentle humour to a story that will resonate with children and pet lovers of all ages.

ISBN 978-1-55017-584-4
paperback / colour illustrations
8" x 8" / 32 pages

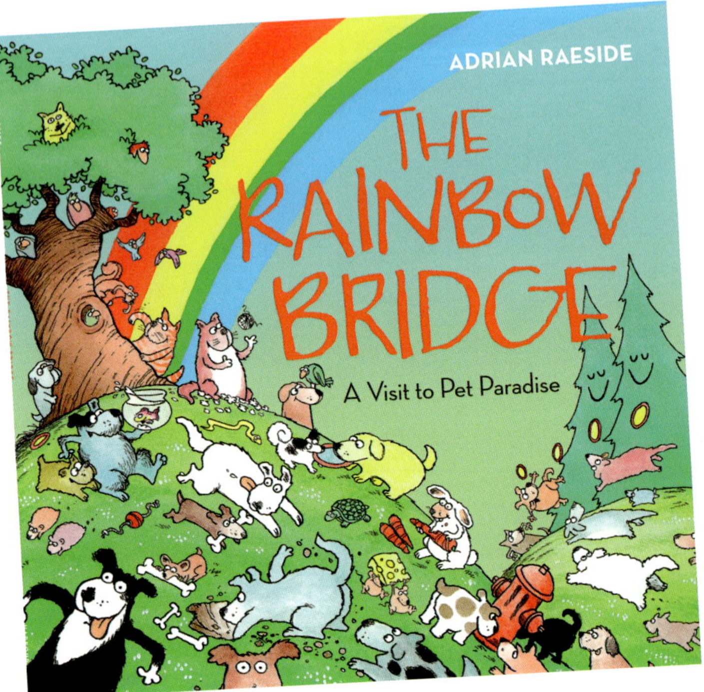

Available at your local bookstore or from

Harbour Publishing
P.O. Box 219
Madeira Park, BC, V0N 2H0
Toll-free order line: 1-800-667-2988

Visit our website for more information on all our titles and authors:
www.harbourpublishing.com

For more laughs visit Adrian Raeside's website:
www.raesidecartoon.com